On the Air!
Listening to Radio Talk

Catherine Sadow
Northeastern University

Edgar Sather
World Learning, Inc.
Brattleboro, Vermont

St. Martin's Press
New York

Editorial Director, ESL/ELT: Tina B. Carver
Assistant Editor: Kimberly Wurtzel
Manager, Publishing Services: Emily Berleth
Associate Editor, Publishing Services: Meryl Gross
Project Management: Books By Design, Inc.
Production Supervisor: Scott Lavelle
Text Design: Books By Design, Inc.
Graphics: Deborah Drummond
Photo Research: Inge King
Cover Design: Evelyn Horovicz
Cover Art: Robert Pizzo

Library of Congress Catalog Card Number: 97-65183

Manufactured in the United States of America.

3 2 1 0 9 8
f e d c b a

For information, write:

St. Martin's Press, Inc.
175 Fifth Avenue
New York, NY 10010

ISBN: 0-312-15405-4

Acknowledgments

Ch. 1, p. 1: Tom and Ray Magliozzi (Click and Clack) from NPR *Car Talk,* courtesy of National Public Radio.
Ch. 2, p. 12: Boy riding bike, Paris, Jaye R. Phillips/The Picture Cube.

Acknowledgments and copyrights are continued at the back of the book on pages 207–208, which constitute an extension of the copyright page.

Contents

CHAPTER 3   *The Common Cold:*
Health Expert Jane Brody Has Some Ideas   **19**

CHAPTER 4   *Are You Game?: Tony from Tyson's Corner*   **30**

Preface

On the Air! Listening to Radio Talk consists of unscripted, natural, unedited listening material from high-interest radio broadcasts, designed for intermediate students (adaptable for advanced students). This book is designed to give intermediate students experience in listening and responding to unedited, natural English speech. And since that speech is usually fraught with linguistic and lexical complexities, it is necessary to prepare students for that listening.

The unique and primary feature of this book is its pre- and post-listening exercises, which make accessible to intermediate students the radio talk that they will be hearing in this course.

Fourteen chapters have been included, more than are usually found in an ESL listening program, as well as a large variety of activities, with the expectation that teachers and students will choose chapters and activities that they are most enthusiastic about and that will lead to student confidence in listening to and understanding authentic English.

The fourteen chapters of this listening program have at their core excerpts from conversations from National Public Radio's *Fresh Air, Morning Edition,* and *Talk of the Nation.* In addition, there are two excerpts from WRKO—The Talk Station and one from *Car Talk.* Two radio advertisements also are included.

We have selected a variety of radio talk to give a cross section of U.S. personalities and the far-ranging issues about which they speak: former president Jimmy Carter talks about the event that inspired a poem he wrote; Chris, a high school student, would like to take time out to ride a bike around the world; rich and famous TV star Roseanne claims that she is still "working-class"; Charlie calls *Car Talk* because he is concerned about a noise in his car's engine.

In each chapter, key vocabulary is introduced through the pre-listening dictation exercises. Additional text is introduced in "Listen Again: Check What You Hear." Then it is recycled in other exercises following the taped conversation. Through these exercises, intermediate students are exposed to and prepared to deal with what is usually considered to be advanced listening material.

Too often students at all levels of English language development tune out completely when listening to language that is "too fast" and "too real" because no one has ever asked them to listen to it. Teachers who have used these materials experimentally in the classroom have found that English-as-Second-Language students can learn to cope with authentic material at an intermediate level and, given appropriate exercises, make good progress toward dealing with unedited speech.

Believing that students will make progress during the semester and that there is varying listening ability within any classroom, we have made an effort to arrange the chapters in order of difficulty. The first five chapters are the easiest; the last three the hardest; those in between are at a medium level of difficulty.

Organization of Chapters

"Introduction" and "Talk It Over"

An introductory reading ("Introduction") sets the stage, introducing the personality and the topic to be highlighted in each chapter. This reading is also on tape.

"Talk It Over" gets students thinking about matters related to the chapter topic as they continue anticipating and being introduced to what they are going to hear. This exercise presents opportunities for rich cross-cultural discussion and observations, when students share their own topic-related knowledge and experience before listening to the tape. For example, here are some questions from Chapter 4: "How did your mother and father meet?" "How do people in your country usually meet the people whom they eventually marry?"

This introduction to the chapter heightens interest in the upcoming conversation.

Pre-Listening Dictations

"First Pre-Listening Dictation" leads to recognition of and familiarity with key vocabulary, phrases, and sentences that the students will be hearing in the conversation. After the students have filled in the blanks with the words they have heard on tape, they attempt to guess the meaning of new words and the sentence as a whole. The teacher assists if necessary.

"Second Pre-Listening Dictation" repeats some of the sentences of the first dictation, sometimes omitting different words to be filled in. If the equipment is available, students then tape these dictation sentences after practicing the pronunciation with the teacher.

Listen to the Conversation

In "Take Notes," students listen to the entire excerpt and make notes of details, words and phrases, and the general gist of the conversation. Some students with limited comprehension may hear only the dictation sentences and little more. After this listening exercise, students review the conversation together, reconstructing as much of the tape as they can.

Listen Again to the Conversation

In "Check What You Hear," students listen to the excerpt again. They have in front of them sentences from the conversation in the order that they appear on the tape, as well as some sentences not contained in the conversation. They check off the sentences as they hear them and follow up this exercise with a discussion. The teacher provides any linguistic or lexical explanations that may be needed.

Check Your Understanding

This section of each chapter gives students an opportunity to assess their comprehension of the conversation.

"True or False" appears in all chapters and in most instances is a listening exercise in which students respond with T (for true) or F (for false) to statements related to information in the conversation.

"Recycling the Information" requires students to choose the correct words or phrases to complete a series of sentences that form short paragraphs. When completed and read together, these paragraphs give a summary of the conversation.

"Recycling Key Vocabulary" is an opportunity for students to demonstrate their understanding of the vocabulary and then use it in a discussion.

"Questions for Discussion" allows students to summarize the information they have heard in the chapter.

Other Exercises

Most chapters include a TOEFL-type multiple-choice exercise on tape using vocabulary from the chapter or information related to it. In almost all of the chapters these exercises include several short conversations, each followed by a question; a longer conversation followed by several questions; or a short lecture followed by several questions.

In some chapters, students are asked to write or record on tape five things they have heard in the conversation.

Some chapters include a choral reading using the idiomatic language of the conversation for the students to recite in pairs or groups. These are on tape.

Other miscellaneous exercises are included in some chapters.

For the Teacher and Transcript

The answer keys for chapter exercises and the transcripts of the conversations are at the back of the book. Students should be encouraged not to look at them until they have finished a chapter. In addition, a separate teacher's manual contains suggestions for teaching and notes about the context and language of each chapter.

Acknowledgments

The authors wish to thank the many people and groups whose cooperation and goodwill have made this book possible.

To the following reviewers of St. Martin's Press, we send our appreciation for their insightful comments and suggestions: Isis C. Clemente, Miami Dade Community College; Gail F. Forman, San Diego City College; Marjorie Friedman, ESL Language Center; and Sally Gearhart, Santa Rosa Junior College.

We are grateful to our editor, Tina Carver, and assistant editor, Kimberly Wurtzel, for their assistance, support, and encouragement. We also want to thank Barbara Jatkola and Herb Nolan for their assistance in the editing and production, respectively, of *On the Air!*.

To Paul McGowan, the media technician at the Northeastern University Library, our appreciation for professional assistance and patience in producing practice tapes for use in the classroom.

Many thanks

to Judy DeFillippo and Jackie Kerstner, who tested chapters in their classrooms;

to Jerome Sadow, who always agreed to be a "second voice" on the many practice tapes;

and to our students, who not only used the material but also were good critics and provided many practical suggestions.

CHAPTER 1

Car Talk The Magliozzi Brothers

What's that strange noise coming from your car's engine? Why does the horn honk when you put your foot on the brake?

If you have a car problem, you can call the weekly radio program of brothers Tom and Ray Magliozzi, and they'll give you their expert opinions about what's wrong.

🔊 Introduction

Can you believe this? One of the most popular radio programs in the United States is about automobile repair. The program is called *Car Talk*. Thousands of people want to know answers to questions such as these: What is that strange engine noise I hear when I'm driving thirty miles per hour? What is the best car to buy in Vermont, where there is a lot of snow in the winter? I've had my car for seven years, and it needs seven hundred dollars' worth of repairs. Is it better to get a new car, or should I go ahead with the repairs?

Men and women from all parts of the United States call to tell the program hosts, Click and Clack, about the problems they are having with their cars. Click and Clack (their real names are Tom and Ray Magliozzi) have had many years of experience repairing cars. They listen to the car problems of the callers and then give their wise advice.

You are going to hear a sample of one of their Saturday morning *Car Talk* programs. Charlie from Los Angeles telephones the radio station to describe a problem he is having with his car. What is the problem? What advice do Click and Clack give? Why do you think the program is so popular?

Talk It Over

DIRECTIONS: In pairs or groups, discuss the following questions.

1. Do you own a car? Is your car important to you? Why?
2. Describe any problems you have had with your car.
3. What do you do when you have a problem with your car? Can you give an example of an experience that either you or a friend has had?

🔊 First Pre-Listening Dictation

DIRECTIONS: The following sentences are from one of the broadcasts of the radio program *Car Talk*. After you fill in the blanks with the words or phrases on the tape, or as your teacher reads the sentences to you, discuss the meaning of each sentence.

1. What's _____, _____?

2. Hangin' in _____. I got a _____. I got a

   _____-_____ Honda.

3. I started experiencing some _____ knocks and some

   _____ in _____ gear.

4. It won't _____ it going up the _____.

5. . . . until you got to _____.

6. It didn't _____.

7. There's something wrong with the _____.

8. I _____ wholeheartedly with my _____.

9. I think your _____'s _____.

10. Get _____ to _____ dealer.

11. No, it's unlikely you did any _____ at _____

    _____ _____.

12. I would tell them the _____ and _____ them

    figure _____ _____.

13. Good _____.

NOW GO OVER THE DICTATION AND DISCUSS THE MEANING OF EACH SENTENCE.

Second Pre-Listening Dictation

DIRECTIONS: These sentences also are from *Car Talk*. After you fill in the blanks with the missing words or phrases as your teacher reads the sentences to you, repeat them aloud. If you have the opportunity, record them on a blank tape.

1. What's _____, man?

2. I _____ a _____-new Honda.

3. _____ got _____ thousand miles on it.

4. I _____ _____ the cheaper gasoline.

5. It was very _____ going up the mountains.

6. _____ it to the _____.

7. Something _____ definitely wrong.

NOW REPEAT THE SENTENCES ALOUD.

📼 Listen to *Car Talk*

Take Notes

DIRECTIONS: You are going to hear a conversation between the hosts of *Car Talk*, Click and Clack, and a caller named Charlie. Take notes on a separate sheet of paper as you listen. Write down main ideas, details, or any words that will help you discuss the conversation.

📼 Listen Again to *Car Talk*

Check What You Hear

DIRECTIONS: Rewind the tape and listen again to Click and Clack's conversation with Charlie. Following are sentences from the tape in the order that you will hear them. There are also some sentences that are not on the tape. Listen carefully, and when you hear one of the sentences, put a check (✓) beside it.

1. ___ You're on *Car Talk*.

2. ___ Thank you. I'm calling for the first time.

3. ___ I got a brand-new Honda.

4. ___ Accord?

5. ___ Just moved out from Chicago.

6. ___ I took it real easy on the car.

7. ___ I didn't go very fast.

8. ___ Go up to the most expensive gas.

9. ___ The problem was . . . when you get into that mountain the air.

10. ___ I was just getting passed by everyone.

11. ___ Despite the fact that it's a brand-new car.

12. ___ Could I already have done damage?

13. ___ Thanks for your help.

DISCUSS THE MEANING OF EACH SENTENCE. THEN GO BACK AND LISTEN AGAIN TO *CAR TALK*.

Write Five Things

DIRECTIONS: Write (or record on your blank tape) five things that you've learned about Charlie and his car, his car problem, and the suggestions of the *Car Talk* **hosts.**

1. _____

_____

_____

2. _____

_____

_____

3. _____

_____

_____

4. _____

_____

_____

5. _____

_____

_____

Check Your Understanding

What did you learn about Charlie's car?

DIRECTIONS: Put a check (✓) beside anything that anyone says *is* wrong with the car or *could be* wrong with the car.

1. ___ There is something wrong with the exhaust system.

2. ___ The radiator is leaking water.

3. ___ The tires are unbalanced.

4. ___ It's burning too much oil.

5. ___ There is a pinging noise.

6. ___ There is a problem with the timing system.

7. ___ It often doesn't have enough power.

8. ___ It won't handle going up hills.

9. ___ The windshield wipers need to be replaced.

10. ___ The brakes don't work well.

🔘 True or False

DIRECTIONS: You will hear eight sentences on tape. Decide whether the sentences are true or false according to the information you have heard on *Car Talk*. Mark T (for true) or F (for false) for each sentence.

1. ___   2. ___   3. ___   4. ___   5. ___   6. ___   7. ___   8. ___

Recycling the Information

DIRECTIONS: Underline the word or phrase in each set of brackets that gives the correct information according to the tape you have heard.

Charlie drove his new [Honda Accord, Toyota, Honda Civic] from [New York City, Chicago, Los Angeles] to [Seattle, Chicago, Los Angeles]. On his journey [east, west, south, north], he had some trouble when he was traveling [on the interstate, in the mountains, along the ocean]. He thinks that perhaps the problem was caused by [the holes in the road, the salty ocean air, the mountain air].

After he arrived in Los Angeles, he had more difficulty with the car. He began to [hear a pinging sound, have trouble with the brakes, have air in the gasoline he used], and he decided to call the radio program *Car Talk*.

The hosts of *Car Talk* listen to his car story and tell him that they think he [bought a bad car, has a real problem, should sell his car immediately]. The hosts agree that the problematic sound in the engine is caused by [mountain air, a timing error, air in the gasoline], and they tell Charlie that he should [drive back to Chicago, see the Honda dealer in Los Angeles, fix the car himself].

After Charlie has listened to the hosts of *Car Talk*, he will probably decide to [sell the car, take it to the dealer in Los Angeles, fix the car himself] because he [doesn't like the car, wants to return to Chicago, agrees with the radio hosts].

Recycling Key Vocabulary

DIRECTIONS: In pairs or groups, explain the meaning of the underlined word(s) in each sentence (a), then explain the meaning of the entire sentence in the context of *Car Talk*. Then answer the follow-up question (b).

1. **Timing**

   a. There's something wrong with the timing.

   b. Give an example of the importance of timing in a sport.

2. **Wholeheartedly**

   a. I agree wholeheartedly with my brother.

   b. Tell about something that you believe wholeheartedly.

3. **To figure out**

   a. Let them figure it out.

   b. Regarding Charlie's car, what do Click and Clack want a mechanic to figure out?

4. **Brand-new**

   a. I got a brand-new Honda.

   b. Do you sometimes buy used things, or must they always be brand-new?

Questions for Discussion

1. The brothers Click and Clack have a theory about what's wrong with Charlie's Honda. What is their theory?

2. After listening to Click and Clack, do you have an idea why their program, *Car Talk*, is so popular?

📼 Short Conversation

DIRECTIONS: Listen to the short conversation on tape, then answer each of the four follow-up questions by circling the letter of the correct answer below.

1. **a.** a garage

   b. her husband

   c. the shopping center

   d. the police

2. **a.** her home

   b. her car

   c. the shopping center

   d. a public pay phone

3. **a.** go home

   b. drive away

   c. walk to the shopping center

   d. wait for the mechanic

4. **a.** It is having an electrical problem.

   b. She has a brand-new car.

   c. She has a flat tire.

   d. She has run out of gas.

🔊 Greetings, Responses, and Farewells

DIRECTIONS: Listen to the greetings, responses, and farewells on tape. Decide whether each of these is formal, informal, or both. Does it mean "Hello"; "How are you?"; "I'm fine"; or "Good-bye"? As you listen, write down the phrase you hear and then put a check (✓) in the box or boxes that best describes it. When you are finished, discuss what you have written and what you have checked.

	Greeting, Response, or Farewell					
	Formal	Informal	Hello	Good-bye	How are you?	I'm fine
1. _____						
2. _____						
3. _____						
4. _____						
5. _____						
6. _____						
7. _____						
8. _____						

📼 Choral Speaking

DIRECTIONS: Listen to the tape and repeat the choral speaking in pairs or groups.

What's Up Stu*?

What's up, man?
Hangin' in there. What's up with you?
I guess I'm hangin' in there, too.

How're you doing?
Takin' it easy. How about you?
Takin' it easy, just like you.

Anything wrong? Something wrong with you?
To tell the truth, I've lost a tooth, and I've got the flu.

You've lost a tooth, you've got the flu?
What can I say! Hang in there, Stu!

*Stu is the derivative of the male name Stuart.

CHAPTER *2*

Taking Time Off

Chris from La Mesa

Chris has a very interesting idea about what he would do if he could take a year off.

📼 Introduction

If you were told that you could take the next year or two and do anything you wanted, what would you do?

One afternoon on the radio program *Talk of the Nation*, the host of the show, Robert Siegel, asked that question this way: "If you could chuck it all, what would you do?" (The expression "chuck it all" means to throw away everything, or, in this case, to take time off—that is, to stop doing what you usually do and have a pleasant change in your routine.)

Several members of the radio audience called the station and gave their answers to this question. One of the people who called was Chris, a student at a junior high school in La Mesa, California. He had a clear idea about what he would like to do if he had the opportunity to take time off. Listen to what he has to say. What do you think about his idea? (In Chapter 12, you will hear what Mike from Rockford, Illinois, said to Robert Siegel.)

Talk It Over

DIRECTIONS: In pairs or groups, discuss the following questions.

1. If you could take time off for a year, what would you want to do?
2. What do you think Chris from La Mesa is going to say?

📼 First Pre-Listening Dictation

DIRECTIONS: The following sentences are from the conversation between Robert Siegel and Chris. After you fill in the blanks with the words or phrases on the tape, or as your teacher reads the sentences to you, discuss the meaning of each sentence.

1. You like _____, I assume.

2. You don't think it would be very, very _____ and

   _____?

3. It would be a _____ to _____ some muscle.

4. Yeah, I should _____.

5. That doesn't _____ you _____?

6. I'd _____ _____ while _____

_____.

NOW GO OVER THE DICTATION AND DISCUSS THE MEANING OF EACH SENTENCE.

Second Pre-Listening Dictation

DIRECTIONS: These sentences also are from the conversation with Chris. After you fill in the blanks with the missing words or phrases as your teacher reads the sentences to you, repeat them aloud. If you have the opportunity, record them on a blank tape.

1. You like biking, _____ _____.

2. It _____ be very, very _____ and wearing.

3. I _____ _____.

4. That doesn't _____ you _____?

NOW REPEAT THE SENTENCES ALOUD.

Listen to Chris

Take Notes

DIRECTIONS: You are going to hear Robert Siegel's radio conversation with Chris. Take notes on a separate sheet of paper as you listen. Write down main ideas, details, or any words that will help you discuss the conversation.

📼 Listen Again to Chris

Check What You Hear

DIRECTIONS: Rewind the tape and listen again to the conversation with Chris. Following are sentences from the tape in the order that you will hear them. There are also some sentences that are not on the tape. Listen carefully, and when you hear one of the sentences, put a check (✓) beside it.

1. ___ You're on the line, I gather, from La Mesa, California.

2. ___ Compare all the different cultures to the United States' culture.

3. ___ Of course, I will need good maps.

4. ___ I would travel between the continents on a boat.

5. ___ No, as long as I got enough sleep and food and water.

6. ___ I probably will sleep in a hotel or a tent.

7. ___ Hear, hear! Would you take anybody along with you?

8. ___ I'm sorry, I missed what you said just a moment ago.

9. ___ And encourage them to do things like that.

DISCUSS THE MEANING OF EACH SENTENCE. THEN GO BACK AND LISTEN AGAIN TO THE CONVERSATION WITH CHRIS.

Check Your Understanding

📼 True or False

DIRECTIONS: You will hear seven sentences on tape. Decide whether the sentences are true or false according to the information you have heard in the conversation with Chris. Mark T (for true) or F (for false) for each sentence.

1. ___   2. ___   3. ___   4. ___   5. ___   6. ___   7. ___

Recycling the Information

DIRECTIONS: Underline the word or phrase in each set of brackets that gives the correct information according to the conversation with Chris.

Chris, who is about [nine, thirteen, twenty] years old, says that if he [had a lot of money, took time off, were older than he is], he would bike [across the ocean, only in Asia, on several continents].

Chris likes this idea for two or three reasons. One reason he gives is that by biking, he could [lose weight, develop his body and strength, gain weight]. Another reason he gives is that in making this trip, he would [learn interesting things, be away from his parents, see beautiful places].

He says that if he went on the trip, he would go [by himself, with his best friend, with several people], and when he returned, he would [sleep for a week, run a marathon, encourage others to make a similar trip].

Recycling Key Vocabulary

DIRECTIONS: In pairs or groups, explain the meaning of the underlined word(s) in each sentence (a), then explain the meaning of the entire sentence in the context of the conversation with Chris. Then answer the follow-up question (b).

1. **To take time off**

   a. I would take time off from school, and bike.

   b. When do you need to take time off?

2. **To assume**

   a. You like biking, I assume.

   b. Sevgin lives in Turkey. Can we assume that he is Turkish?

3. **Tiring and wearing**

   a. You don't think it would be very, very tiring and wearing?

   b. Tell about an activity that is tiring and wearing for you.

4. **To gain some muscle**

    a. It would be a chance to <u>gain some muscle</u>.

    b. If you wanted to gain some muscle, how would you do it?

5. **To scare off**

    a. That doesn't <u>scare</u> you <u>off</u>?

    b. Would bad weather scare you off from a camping trip?

6. **Chance**

    a. It would be a <u>chance</u> to gain some muscle.

    b. If you had a chance to fly to the moon, would you do it?

Questions for Discussion

1. If Chris actually made this trip, what are some of the things and places he would probably see?

2. What are the most important things he would learn if he made the trip? What do you think about his idea?

Short Conversations

DIRECTIONS: Listen to the five short conversations on tape, then answer each of the follow-up questions by circling the letter of the correct answer below.

1. **a.** He doesn't need a vacation.

    b. He doesn't want time off.

    c. He needs to earn the money.

    d. He wants a new job.

2. **a.** Peter's boss

    b. Peter's grandmother

    c. Peter

    d. the company

3. **a.** in the fall

   b. in the winter

   c. in the spring

   d. in July

4. **a.** take a bus

   b. run

   c. walk

   d. go to a basketball game

5. **a.** in a theater

   b. in a kitchen

   c. in a store

   d. in a car

CHAPTER 3

The Common Cold

Health Expert Jane Brody Has Some Ideas

Jane Brody, health expert, writes about health for the New York Times. *Hear what she has to say on the subject of the common cold.*

It is strange, isn't it, that in this day and age, when doctors, researchers, and scientists have been able to discover cures for so many diseases, no cure has yet been found for the common cold. Yes, we can buy many drugstore medicines that claim to reduce the symptoms of the common cold, but often when we catch a cold, we are sick for one to two weeks or more, even if we are using these medicines.

How can you avoid catching a cold? Drink a lot of orange juice? Stay away from crowds of people? Never go outside with wet hair? Don't eat ice cream? Everyone seems to have a favorite theory.

And if you catch a cold, how can you get well quickly? Many people say that chicken soup is the best medicine. Others may tell you to take aspirin; drink a mixture of hot water, honey, and garlic; take a hot bath; or go to bed early. What about the often quoted remedy "Starve a cold, feed a fever"?

In this interview, Jane Brody, who writes about health for the *New York Times*, talks about the common cold. She shares her ideas about how we get a cold and perhaps how we can prevent it. After you have listened to what she has to say, perhaps you will be better able to keep yourself from catching a cold. What do you think?

Talk It Over

DIRECTIONS: In pairs or groups, discuss the following questions.

1. Do you often get a cold or the flu in winter? If you do, describe how you feel.
2. How do you think people catch a cold or the flu?
3. When you have a cold or the flu, what things do you do to cure yourself?
4. Are there any special things that are used in your country or in your family to cure a cold or the flu?

📼 First Pre-Listening Dictation

DIRECTIONS: The following sentences are from Terry Gross's interview with Jane Brody. After you fill in the blanks with the words or phrases on the tape, or as your teacher reads the sentences to you, discuss the meaning of each sentence.

1. How _____ this winter _____ for you

   _____ _____?

2. I think we tend to _____ ourselves.

3. _____ and _____ viruses are rampant.

4. Everyone around you _____ to be coughing and

   _____.

5. Vitamin C . . . does seem to be able to _____ many colds.

6. [Vitamin C seems to] _____ the symptoms of many colds.

7. This was very _____ to him.

8. My _____.

NOW GO OVER THE DICTATION AND DISCUSS THE MEANING OF EACH SENTENCE.

Second Pre-Listening Dictation

DIRECTIONS: These sentences also are from the interview with Jane Brody. After you fill in the blanks with the missing words or phrases as your teacher reads the sentences to you, repeat them aloud. If you have the opportunity, record them on a blank tape.

1. How _____ this winter _____ for you so far?

2. We _____ to push ourselves.

3. _____ and cold _____ are _____.

4. My _____.

NOW REPEAT THE SENTENCES ALOUD.

📼 Listen to Jane Brody

Take Notes

DIRECTIONS: You are going to hear Terry Gross's interview with Jane Brody. Take notes on a separate sheet of paper as you listen. Write down main ideas, details, or any words that will help you discuss the interview.

📼 Listen Again to Jane Brody

Check What You Hear

DIRECTIONS: Rewind the tape and listen again to the interview with Jane Brody. Following are sentences from the tape in the order that you will hear them. There are also some sentences that are not on the tape. Listen carefully, and when you hear one of the sentences, put a check (✓) beside it.

1. ____ Busy, very busy, and I try very hard in the winter to get a little bit of extra sleep.

2. ____ You are exposed to all these people who may be carrying organisms.

3. ____ Colds are very often spread hand to hand.

4. ____ Take many hot baths in the wintertime.

5. ____ Although [eyes are] not an infected site, they are a conduit into the nasal passages.

6. ___ You can transfer the cold virus to your eye.

7. ___ You get a cold just simply from having scratched your eye.

8. ___ Do not travel on a crowded train or bus.

9. ___ This is another trick I have for flying.

10. ___ I take vitamin C in a large dose before I fly.

11. ___ You can buy vitamin C in most drugstores.

12. ___ You are just as likely to be infected with or without vitamin C.

13. ___ Why take a chance if you can get rid of the symptoms fast?

14. ___ I think that's the better part of valor.

15. ___ The former head of the Federal Aviation Agency had this problem of getting pneumonia.

16. ___ I wish you good health.

DISCUSS THE MEANING OF EACH SENTENCE. THEN GO BACK AND LISTEN AGAIN TO THE INTERVIEW WITH JANE BRODY.

Write Five Things

DIRECTIONS: Write (or record on your blank tape) five things you've learned about colds from the interview with Jane Brody.

1. _____

   _____

   _____

2. _____

   _____

   _____

3. _____

_____

_____

4. _____

_____

_____

5. _____

_____

_____

Check Your Understanding

True or False

DIRECTIONS: Decide whether the following seven sentences are true or false according to the information you have heard in the interview with Jane Brody. Mark T (for true) or F (for false) for each sentence.

1. ___ Brody has not been busy this winter.

2. ___ You should get more sleep in the wintertime.

3. ___ Washing your hands causes colds.

4. ___ Taking vitamin C always prevents colds.

5. ___ Vitamin C works for everybody and for all colds.

6. ___ It is important to drink liquids.

7. ___ If you have a cold, don't fly on a plane.

Recycling the Information

DIRECTIONS: Underline the word or phrase in each set of brackets that gives the correct information according to the tape you have heard.

Jane Brody writes about [sports, health, movies] in the *New York Times*. In the interview with her, Terry Gross asks her how her winter has been. Brody answers that she has been very [happy, tired, busy]. In her answer, she explains that she thinks that in the wintertime, many people usually don't [keep warm enough, get enough sleep, eat enough], and therefore they can more easily [be cold, catch cold, be hungry]. She suggests that it is a good idea in the wintertime to [wear extra clothing, eat more food, get extra sleep].

She also has other suggestions for preventing colds. She thinks it is very important to wash your [hands, face, clothes] after you [go to the bathroom, shake hands with someone, have been on a plane or train] because the cold virus can easily travel from your [hands, clothes, shoes] to your [ears, eyes, cheeks], and then you can become [infected, tired, hungry] and catch a cold.

She suggests [drinking, sneezing, coughing] more and also taking large doses of [medicine, vitamin C, aspirin] before flying on a plane or riding on a bus. She says that if you follow this advice, you can [stop completely, prevent, shorten] the symptoms of a cold.

A friend of hers had a problem when he [traveled in the wintertime, flew on airplanes, rode on trains]. When he traveled, he would usually get [jet lag, pneumonia, flu], and she suggested that he [stop traveling by plane, eat different foods, take vitamin C]. The result is that her friend now [drinks more coffee, drives to work in his car, is healthier].

Recycling Key Vocabulary

DIRECTIONS: In pairs or groups, explain the meaning of the underlined word(s) in each sentence (a), then explain the meaning of the entire sentence in the context of the interview with Jane Brody. Then answer the follow-up question (b).

1. **Tend to**

   a. I think we <u>tend to</u> push ourselves.

   b. Do you tend to speak very quickly when you are nervous?

2. **Under those circumstances**

    a. <u>Under those circumstances</u> . . . I take vitamin C.

    b. Under what circumstances do you get angry?

3. **Trick**

    a. Another <u>trick</u> I have for flying is I take vitamin C.

    b. What tricks do you know for learning English well?

Questions for Discussion

1. Summarize what Jane Brody says about preventing colds.

2. How many diseases can you think of that spread from person to person? How do these diseases spread? How many diseases can you think of that are *not* spread from person to person?

📼 Short Conversations

DIRECTIONS: Listen to the seven short conversations on tape, then answer each of the follow-up questions by circling the letter of the correct answer below.

1. **a.** in the winter

    b. all year round

    c. in the summer

    d. at the ski lodge

2. **a.** She wants him to come to dinner.

    b. She wants him to wash the dishes.

    c. She wants him to wash his hands.

    d. She wants to give him orders.

3. **a.** about six and a half hours

    b. about five and a half hours

    c. about six hours

    d. less than usual

4. **a.** the woman's cold

   b. a cold or the flu

   c. a bottle of vitamin C

   d. an old clue

5. **a.** The food is Italian.

   b. There are few people there.

   b. There are a lot of people there.

   d. The service is not good.

6. **a.** Go by train.

   b. Go by bus.

   c. Travel by plane.

   d. Stay at home.

7. **a.** She is feeling well.

   b. She has visited the doctor.

   c. She thinks she has the flu.

   d. She has the flu.

Thank You and Good-bye

Terry Gross says to Jane Brody, "Well, Jane Brody, I wish you good health."

Brody replies, "Thank you, and the same to you."

We often use "Thank you, and the same to you" as a response.

Example: "Merry Christmas."
               "Thank you, and the same to you."

Terry Gross also thanks Brody for being interviewed, and Brody says, "My pleasure." This is very polite and formal. She could have said, "You're welcome." If she wanted to be very informal, she might have said, "It was no big deal."

1. The president of the university: "Thank you for coming to speak to our graduates."

   The speaker: "_____"

2. "Happy New Year"

   "_____"

3. "Hey, Joe, thanks for helping me move."

   "_____"

4. "Can you tell me the time?"
   "It's four-fifteen."
   "Thank you."

   "_____"

Note: What do you think is the most common response to someone who says "Thank you"? Is it "You're welcome"? Listen carefully to what people say. Many people say "Thank *you*!" When you listen to the radio or watch television, notice what people say when someone says "Thank you" to them. For example, almost everyone to whom Terry Gross (on the radio program *Fresh Air*) says, "Thank you for being on the show today," responds with, "Thank *you*! [for having me, asking me, inviting me, and so on]." See if you can figure out when it is better to say "You're welcome" and when to say "Thank *you*." Listen for examples of this phenomenon during the next week.

🎧 Choral Speaking

DIRECTIONS: Listen to the tape and repeat the choral speaking in pairs or groups.

Blowing, Coughing, Sneezing

Blowing, coughing, sneezing.
Blowing, coughing, sneezing.

What's the matter with you?
What's the matter with you?

What's the matter with me?
What's the matter with me?
I have a cold; I have the flu!

You have a cold? You have the flu?
I have some chicken soup for you.
Chicken soup and vitamin C:
Old and modern remedies.

Blowing, coughing, sneezing.
You are such a treasure!

No, no. Not another word.
It's entirely my pleasure.

CHAPTER 4

Are You Game?

Tony from Tyson's Corner

If you think that it's crazy to try to find a best friend (or lover) by answering an advertisement on the radio, then you'll think that Tony is crazy.

But perhaps you think it's a good idea to advertise for friendship or love. If so, read on.

🔊 Introduction

Personal ads in newspapers and on the radio (as you will soon hear) are becoming a more and more popular way to meet people in the United States. You are going to hear an example of a radio show, aired on Valentine's Day, on which people place advertisements for themselves.

In this edition of a radio program called *Talk of the Nation*, we hear the personal ad of a young woman who is hoping to get a response from a man (or men) listening to the program. Then we hear the response of a man who calls the radio station because he is interested in this woman.

The host begins the program by saying, "I'm going to be reading some personal ads, playing others through the course of the program. If you're game, if the person in the ad sounds like the person you've been looking for, give us a call. We'll try to hook you up before the hour is out."

What do you think about this way of meeting people—maybe even a future husband or wife? After you have listened to this program, perhaps you will change your mind, perhaps not. But try to keep an open mind.

Talk It Over

DIRECTIONS: In pairs or groups, discuss the following questions.

1. How did your mother and father meet?
2. Tell one of your favorite stories about how two people met and then fell in love (perhaps from a book, movie, or TV program or from your own personal story). Tell where and when they met and describe other details of the meeting.
3. How do people in your country usually meet the people they eventually marry?

🔊 First Pre-Listening Dictation

DIRECTIONS: The following sentences are from a conversation between the host of a radio show and a caller named Tony, from Tyson's Corner, Virginia. After you fill in the blanks with the words or phrases on the tape, or as your teacher reads the sentences to you, discuss the meaning of each sentence.

1. If _____ _____ . . . give us a call.

2. We'll try to hook _____ up before the _____ is

    _____ .

3. Affectionate and _____, _____ and pragmatic.

4. Are you _____ the _____ for our young woman?

5. [It's] getting _____ and _____ every day.

6. I guess _____ just don't have the _____ anymore.

7. Do you _____ what I _____?

NOW GO OVER THE DICTATION AND DISCUSS THE MEANING OF EACH
SENTENCE.

Second Pre-Listening Dictation

DIRECTIONS: These sentences also are from the conversation between the
radio host and Tony. After you fill in the blanks with the missing words or
phrases as your teacher reads the sentences to you, repeat them aloud. If you
have the opportunity, record them on a blank tape.

1. If you're _____ . . . give us a call.

2. Are you _____ _____ _____ for our

    young woman?

3. [It's] getting _____ and _____ every day.

NOW REPEAT THE SENTENCES ALOUD.

📼 Listen to "Are You Game?"

Take Notes

DIRECTIONS: You are going to hear the conversation between the radio host and Tony. Take notes on a separate sheet of paper as you listen. Write down main ideas, details, or any words that will help you discuss the conversation.

Following is the text of the personal ad that you will hear at the beginning of the radio show.

> Attractive, fit, with long dark hair, single white female, thirty-one, writer. Affectionate and honest, daring and pragmatic. Enjoys eclectic conversation, hiking, bodies of water, film and blues music. Seeks stable, intelligent, affectionate man twenty-nine to thirty-eight with vital spirit, who enjoys work and play, independence and partnership.

📼 Listen Again to "Are You Game?"

Check What You Hear

DIRECTIONS: Rewind the tape and listen again to the conversation between the radio host and Tony. Following are sentences from the tape in the order that you will hear them. There are also some sentences that are not on the tape. Listen carefully, and when you hear one of the sentences, put a check (✓) beside it.

1. ___ Are you game?

2. ___ I listen to the radio every Sunday morning.

3. ___ Tell us about yourself.

4. ___ Well, over the long haul.

5. ___ Oh, was born in Iran.

6. ___ I came to find the ideal woman.

7. ___ The ideal woman is very beautiful.

8. ___ It's one of the fastest-growing parts of Virginia.

9. ___ I guess people just don't have the trust anymore.

10. ___ I guess it's not a big staff.

11. ___ I have a lot of free time.

12. ___ I mean, you put in a lot of hours.

13. ___ I'm just kind of tired of the, like, bar scene.

14. ___ And did anything stick out for you about that ad?

15. ___ I didn't realize how much people are willing to sort of really put themselves out on the line.

16. ___ I don't know if I'm self-confident enough to do that. Gee, am I?

17. ___ It's hard.

DISCUSS THE MEANING OF EACH SENTENCE. THEN GO BACK AND LISTEN AGAIN TO THE CONVERSATION WITH TONY.

Write Five Things

DIRECTIONS: Write (or record on your blank tape) five things you've learned about Tony.

1. _____

_____

_____

2. _____

_____

_____

3. _____

_____

_____

4. _____

_____

_____

5. _____

_____

_____

Check Your Understanding

🔊 True or False

DIRECTIONS: You will hear seven sentences on tape. Decide whether the sentences are true or false according to the information you have heard in the conversation with Tony. Mark T (for true) or F (for false) for each sentence.

1. ___   2. ___   3. ___   4. ___   5. ___   6. ___   7. ___

Recycling the Information

DIRECTIONS: Underline the word or phrase in each set of brackets that gives the correct information according to the conversation with Tony.

"Personal Ads" is a radio show for people who want to meet other people. On Valentine's Day, a [single, married, divorced] white female (SWF) calls the radio program and says that she wants to meet [a very tall, a very handsome, an affectionate] man. Tony, who is [a doctor, a consultant, an engineer] and is [eighteen, forty-five, thirty-eight] years old, hears this personal ad, and he telephones the station.

We learn that Tony moved to the United States from [Ireland, Iraq, Iran] about [thirty-eight, twenty, five] years ago and currently lives in [Vermont, Virginia, Washington]. He works for [his brother, his father, himself]. He says that he still hopes that he can find [a pretty, the ideal, a well-educated] woman.

According to what he says, Tony has looked for this woman for many years and in many places, including [bars, Iran, committee meetings]. He says that it is becoming tougher and tougher for him to meet women because he is [very busy, not handsome, over thirty-five years old]. When Ray asks him why he chose to call the woman in this ad, Tony mentions her [education, age, good qualities].

Ray, the host of the show, thinks it must be very [easy, hard, enjoyable] to call the show. Why does he think this?

Recycling Key Vocabulary

DIRECTIONS: In pairs or groups, explain the meaning of the underlined word(s) in each sentence (a), then explain the meaning of the entire sentence in the context of the conversation with Tony. Then answer the follow-up question (b).

1. **On the lookout**

   a. Are you on the lookout for our young woman?

   b. When Jane goes shopping, she's always on the lookout for bargains. What about you?

2. **Over the long haul**

   a. Where are you from . . . over the long haul?

   b. Over the long haul, will English be important to you? Why?

3. **Tougher and tougher**

   a. Yes, getting tougher and tougher every day.

   b. What gets tougher and tougher for Tony? What about you?

4. **Trust**

   a. People just don't have the trust anymore.

   b. Whom do you trust and why?

5. **To be game**

   a. If you're game . . . give us a call.

   b. Are you game for very strenuous physical exercise?

6. **To stick out**

   a. Did anything stick out for you?

   b. What sticks out in your memory about your elementary school days?

7. **Self-confident**

   a. I don't know if I'm self-confident enough to do that.

   b. Are you a self-confident person? In what ways?

Questions for Discussion

1. What do you think about this type of radio program? Does a program like this one exist in your country? Would you ever consider using a dating service like this?

2. What is the host's reaction to Tony's call? Why does he say "AYYYIYI" just after Tony hangs up the phone?

3. Tony says that he is "tired of the bar scene." What does he mean?

4. Put yourself in the position of the single white female who placed this personal ad on the radio. Do you think she will be interested in meeting Tony? Why or why not?

5. Would you be interested in meeting Tony? Why or why not? In meeting the single white female? Why or why not?

Personal Ads

DIRECTIONS: Listen to the following ads on tape. Fill in the blanks with the missing words. Discuss the ads and then see whether you can decide who might be a good match based on the information in the ads.

Women Seeking Men

Number One. One more try: Attractive, _____, SWF (single white female), twenty-four, with bright _____ seeks nice guy to _____ coffee, ocean, _____, Sundays, music, Boston.

Number Two. Attractive, tall, SWF, twenty-four, _____ hair, _____ eyes, outgoing, sincere, _____ skiing, _____ activities. Seeks honest SM, twenty-four to thirty.

Number Three. Asian physician. _____ attractive SF, thirty-three, five foot three inches, one hundred ten pounds, loves _____. Seeking professional successful male, thirty to forty.

Number Four. Asian-American _____ reporter, one in a million! _____ professional, successful man of integrity, thirty-nine-plus, thinks big with a _____ heart.

Number Five. Active, attractive, fit DWF (divorced white female), forty-five, varied _____, including sports, travel, _____, movies. Seeking mate, forty-two to _____, N/S (nonsmoker).

Number Six. Animals/nature lover wants _____ friend, DWF, sixty, has owned/studied domestic/zoo _____: _____ to _____.

Men Seeking Women

Number One. True gentleman. DWM, forty-six (look thirty something), five feet eight inches, one hundred seventy pounds, N/S, _____, affectionate. Like animals, dining out, _____, movies, _____. Seek _____, down-to-earth S/DWF, thirty-three to thirty-nine, for fun, adventure, and travel.

Number Two. SWM, twenty-four, five feet seven inches, athletic, slim, _____, comfortable, open-minded. Seeks petite SWF, twenty to twenty-six.

Number Three. Asian woman _____ by SWM five feet nine inches. Handsome Omar Sharif look-alike, Italian, fit, great _____, _____. Need F soulmate.

Number Four. Very attractive, honest, stable, _____ SWM, forty, six feet, one hundred eighty pounds, physically in _____ _____, enjoys hiking, racquetball, theater, et cetera. Seeks very attractive SWF, thirty-two to thirty-eight, who is professionally employed, educated, and _____ in working on a long-term relationship leading to marriage and a _____.

Number Five. DWM, sixty (looks fifty), five feet six inches, seeks DWF, attractive, passionate, _____, kind. Love movies, _____ out, and cuddling.

Number Six. Straightforward, sincere, _____ businessman, athletic with eclectic interests, seeks independent, interesting lady, _____ to _____.

CHAPTER 5

Standing on the Moon

Alan Shepard, Astronaut

On February 4, 1971, Alan Shepard walked on the moon. As he looked up at the earth, what did he see? What did he think about?

💿 Introduction

On February 4, 1971, Alan Shepard, commander of the *Apollo 14* space mission, became the fifth person to walk on the moon. He and fellow astronaut Edgar Mitchell spent nine hours and twenty-three minutes in space suits on the lunar surface. Their major job was to gather and photograph samples of the materials on the moon's surface, including rocks and stones, to take back to geologists on earth.

When he was asked about his lunar experience, Mitchell said, "What it did for me is really force me to get a picture of the universe from a totally different perspective and then start to question our conventional ways of looking at ourselves, our place in the universe, our place in life, what it's all about."

A year and a half earlier, on July 20, 1969, the astronauts of *Apollo 11* had made the first landing on the moon. At that time, Commander Neil Armstrong was the first person to walk on the moon. As he took his first step out of the lunar module, he radioed these words to the earth: "That's one small step for a man; one giant leap for mankind."

In a July 1994 interview with a writer for the *New York Times*, Alan Shepard talked about looking at earth: "I remember being struck by the fact that it looks so peaceful from that distance, but remembering on the other hand all the confrontation going on all over that planet and feeling a little sad that people on planet Earth couldn't see that same sight because obviously all the military and political differences become so insignificant seeing it from the distance."

In the interview with Alan Shepard that you will hear on the radio program *Fresh Air*, he reminisces with Terry Gross about his adventure on the moon.

Talk It Over

DIRECTIONS: In pairs or groups, discuss the following questions.

1. Are you concerned about the earth? What are your concerns?
2. Are there things occurring in your country that could affect the planet?
3. Do you believe that there will be outer space travel soon?

4. Explain what Neil Armstrong meant in his message to the people on earth.

5. If you had a chance to stand on the moon, what do you think your thoughts and feelings would be?

🔊 First Pre-Listening Dictation

DIRECTIONS: The following sentences are from Terry Gross's interview with Alan Shepard. After you fill in the blanks with the words or phrases on the tape, or as your teacher reads the sentences to you, discuss the meaning of each sentence.

1. I don't think we had any _____ about the actual

   _____ of the moon—about the barrenness.

2. We knew the _____ configuration of where the craters were

   _____ to be.

3. You can see _____ on the ice caps on the _____

   Pole, _____ _____ _____.

4. It's just an _____, _____ view.

5. You know, _____ _____ we think _____

   infinite.

6. _____ a _____ those folks _____

   _____ can't get _____ together.

7. [People] have to think about trying to _____, to save what

   _____ resources they have.

8. I actually shed a _____ of _____.

NOW GO OVER THE DICTATION AND DISCUSS THE MEANING OF EACH SENTENCE.

Second Pre-Listening Dictation

DIRECTIONS: These sentences also are from the interview with Alan Shepard. After you fill in the blanks with the missing words or phrases as your teacher reads the sentences to you, repeat them aloud. If you have the opportunity, record them on a blank tape.

1. We had looked at _____ of our landing site.

2. The _____ is totally _____.

3. We think it's _____.

4. We don't _____ about resources.

5. I actually _____ a couple of _____.

NOW REPEAT THE SENTENCES ALOUD.

🔊 Listen to Alan Shepard

Take Notes

DIRECTIONS: You are going to hear Terry Gross's interview with Alan Shepard. Take notes on a separate sheet of paper as you listen. Write down main ideas, details, or any words that will help you discuss the interview.

🔊 Listen Again to Alan Shepard

Check What You Hear

DIRECTIONS: Rewind the tape and listen again to the interview with Alan Shepard. Following are sentences from the tape in the order that you will hear them. There are also some sentences that are not on the tape. Listen carefully, and when you hear one of the sentences, put a check (✓) beside it.

1. ___ We had looked at pictures of our landing site taken by previous missions.

2. ___ We had worked with models that were made from those pictures.

3. ___ The surface of the moon is strange.

4. ___ You have a blue ocean(s) and the brown landmasses—the brown continents.

5. ___ It looks like it—it does have limits.

6. ___ It's a little fragile.

7. ___ I thought about staying on the moon and living there.

8. ___ And it's just very emotional.

DISCUSS THE MEANING OF EACH SENTENCE. THEN GO BACK AND LISTEN AGAIN TO THE INTERVIEW WITH ALAN SHEPARD.

Check Your Understanding

🔘 True or False

DIRECTIONS: You will hear six sentences on tape. Decide whether the sentences are true or false according to the information you have heard in the interview with Alan Shepard. Mark T (for true) or F (for false) for each sentence.

1. ___   2. ___   3. ___   4. ___   5. ___   6. ___

Recycling the Information

DIRECTIONS: Underline the word or phrase in each set of brackets that gives the correct information according to the chapter introduction and the interview with Alan Shepard.

Astronaut Alan Shepard was the commander of the *Apollo 14* mission to the moon, and he was the [first, third, fifth] human being to walk on its surface. He says that the surface of the moon is [barren, black, blue], which was [a surprise, not a surprise, very exciting] because he [hadn't

expected to see colors, had studied models of the surface, had made photographs of the moon's surface] before beginning this mission.

When he looked at the earth, he could see [blue, green, brown] landmasses, [blue, black, white] sky, and [brown, green, blue] oceans. He said that from the moon, the earth looks [bigger than, about the same size as, smaller than] the moon looks from the earth. He also mentioned seeing the ice caps of the [North Pole, oceans, South Pole].

While he stood on the surface of the moon, he saw that the earth looked very [barren, colorless, fragile]. That sight also made him realize that the people on the earth need to [create a global government and economy, be more careful about their resources, save the ice caps]. Before leaving the moon, he became emotional about [*Apollo 14*, the fragile earth, the barren moon].

Recycling Key Vocabulary

DIRECTIONS: In pairs or groups, explain the meaning of the underlined word(s) in each sentence (a), then explain the meaning of the entire sentence in the context of the interview with Alan Shepard. Then answer the follow-up question (b).

1. **To be supposed to**

   a. We knew . . . where the craters were <u>supposed to</u> be.

   b. How are you supposed to act in a movie theater in your country?

2. **Chance**

   a. . . . having a <u>chance</u> to rest a little bit.

   b. What do you like to do for recreation when you have a chance?

3. **To get along**

   a. It's a shame those folks down there can't <u>get along</u> together.

   b. If you don't get along with someone, what are the reasons?

4. **To shed a tear**

   a. I actually <u>shed a couple of tears</u> looking up at the earth.

   b. Can you remember the last time you shed a tear?

Questions for Discussion

1. Summarize what Alan Shepard saw from the surface of the moon.
2. Shepard said that he "shed tears" on the moon. What reason does he give for crying?
3. What made the biggest impressions on him as he stood on the moon?

📼 Short Conversations

DIRECTIONS: Listen to the five short conversations on tape, then answer each of the follow-up questions by circling the letter of the correct answer below.

1. **a.** Central Park
   b. friendly people
   c. nothing
   d. tall buildings

2. **a.** to a hospital
   b. to a baseball game
   c. to a home for old men
   d. to a theater

3. **a.** on the earth
   b. in an ocean
   c. in Africa
   d. on the moon

4. **a.** because they need handkerchiefs
   b. because the movie is sad
   c. because they like movies
   d. because the movie is funny

5. **a.** go to a small town
   b. live in a big city
   c. get married
   d. live with the man's family

CHAPTER 6

Two Radio Ads

Cellular Phones and Airlines

Salespeople need to persuade us that what they are selling is "better" or "the best." Radio programs are sponsored by companies that want us to buy their products. Here are two examples.

📟 Introduction

In this chapter, you are going to hear typical radio advertisements (ads) for two different products: cellular phones and an airline. In these very short commercials, the ad writer has very little time to get the selling message across, sometimes only about ten seconds, and never more than a minute, so the writer needs to be very efficient and economical in his or her use of words. And, of course, the writer needs to be very persuasive in what he or she says about the product so that we, the potential buyers, will be convinced that we should buy it.

How do ad writers do this? For one thing, they frequently use words that end with *er*, such as bigger, better, or cheaper, or in words that end with *est*, such as biggest, best, or cheapest.

As you listen to these radio ads, listen especially for the selling points (advantages) of each product. What are the unique, extraordinary, or unusual characteristics of the products that the writers hope will cause us to run out and shop for them?

When you have finished listening to the two commercials, try to make a list of the most interesting selling points that are typically used in radio (and magazine, newspaper, and TV) ads.

1. Cellular Phones

Talk It Over

DIRECTIONS: In pairs or groups, discuss the following questions.

1. Do you have a cellular phone? Do you think you would want to have a cellular phone? How and when might you use it?
2. If you were selling cellular phones, what would be your selling points? After you have heard the ad, compare your own selling points with those of the advertiser.
3. Tell about one of the best bargains you have ever heard of.
4. Are you good at bargaining? When have you bargained? At what stores or businesses in your own country or in the United States is it appropriate to bargain? Where is it not appropriate to bargain?

🔊 First Pre-Listening Dictation

DIRECTIONS: The following sentences are from the advertisement for cellular phones. After you fill in the blanks with the words or phrases on the tape, or as your teacher reads the sentences to you, discuss the meaning of each sentence.

1. The question today is _____ _____

   _____ to get a cellular _____, but where.

2. An off-the-shelf _____-basement phone won't look like

   much of a _____ when _____ in need of

   _____ and you can't get it.

3. So keep it _____ and call Phil DePalma at _____-

   _____-_____-_____.

4. Right now, get a _____ and transportable phone

   _____ with antenna, carrying case, and _____

   lighter adapter for only _____, a _____ of

   _____ _____ Phil's everyday price.

NOW GO OVER THE DICTATION AND DISCUSS THE MEANING OF EACH SENTENCE.

Second Pre-Listening Dictation

DIRECTIONS: These sentences also are from the ad for cellular phones. After you fill in the blanks with the missing words or phrases as your teacher reads the sentences to you, repeat them aloud. If you have the opportunity, record them on a blank tape.

1. What a _____.

2. Keep it _____.

NOW REPEAT THE SENTENCES ALOUD.

🔊 Listen to the Cellular Phone Ad

Take Notes

DIRECTIONS: You are going to hear the radio advertisement for cellular phones. Take notes on a separate sheet of paper as you listen. Write down main ideas, details, or any words that will help you discuss the ad.

🔊 Listen Again to the Cellular Phone Ad

Check What You Hear

DIRECTIONS: Rewind the tape and listen again to the ad for cellular phones. Following are sentences from the tape in the order that you will hear them. There are also some sentences that are not on the tape. Listen carefully, and when you hear one of the sentences, put a check (✓) beside it.

1. ___ It can seem like a difficult decision.

2. ___ Phil DePalma's Cellular Mobile Communications.

3. ___ An authorized Cellular One agent is the choice.

4. ___ There is no other.

5. ___ Phil's people don't sell TVs or two-by-fours.

6. ___ Keep it simple and call Phil DePalma.

7. ___ Right now, get a unit and transportable phone.

8. ___ Call as quickly as you can.

9. ___ You can now enjoy the safety and convenience of a cellular phone.

DISCUSS THE MEANING OF EACH SENTENCE. THEN GO BACK AND LISTEN AGAIN TO THE AD FOR CELLULAR PHONES.

🎧 How Well Do You Hear Numbers?

DIRECTIONS: In this exercise, listen to the tape for prices and numbers. Put a check (✓) beside the price or number that you hear.

1. ___ $29.99 **or** ___ $29.29

2. ___ $40 **or** ___ $14

3. ___ $111 **or** ___ $1,100

4. ___ 50 cents off **or** ___ 15 cents off

5. ___ A savings of $70 **or** ___ a savings of $17

6. ___ Call 1-800-499-3900 **or** ___ Call 1-800-499-3700

7. ___ Area code 212-361-2121 **or** ___ Area code 312-361-2121

8. ___ There's a 15 percent discount **or** ___ There's a 50 percent discount

9. ___ The speed limit is 55 miles an hour **or** ___ The speed limit is 65 miles an hour

10. ___ For further information, call 373-2455 **or** ___ For further information, call 363-2455

Check Your Understanding

True or False

DIRECTIONS: Decide whether the following seven sentences are true or false according to the information you have heard in the ad for cellular phones. Mark T (for true) or F (for false) for each sentence.

1. ___ It is difficult to find a place to buy a cellular phone today in the United States.

2. ___ Phil DePalma doesn't sell TV sets.

3. ___ Phil's sale price for the cellular phone is about thirty dollars.

4. ___ Phil usually sells cellular phones for about two hundred dollars.

5. ___ If you buy the phone now at Phil DePalma's, you'll also get a free cigarette lighter adapter.

6. ___ Cellular phones have many advantages, but they are not convenient.

7. ___ Phil says that he will repair your phone if you have trouble with it.

Recycling Key Vocabulary

DIRECTIONS: In pairs or groups, explain the meaning of the underlined word(s) in each sentence (a), then explain the meaning of the entire sentence in the context of the ad for cellular phones. Then answer the follow-up question (b).

1. **Authorized**
   a. An authorized Cellular One agent is the choice.
   b. In your country, who is authorized to perform weddings?

2. **Leading**
   a. You'll be on Cellular One, New England's leading network.
   b. What is the leading brand of toothpaste in your country?

3. **Bargain**
   a. [It] won't look like much of a bargain when you're in need of service and you can't get it.
   b. What kind of bargains do you look for? Where?

Questions for Discussion

1. The advertisement gives several selling points of the product. What are they?

2. Evaluate the advertisement you have heard. What are its strengths and weaknesses? Is it convincing? After hearing the ad, do you want to buy a cellular phone? Would you buy it from Phil? Why or why not?

🔊 Choral Speaking

DIRECTIONS: Listen to the tape and repeat the choral speaking in pairs or groups.

A Real Bargain!

What great shoes! What great shoes! I love them! I love them!
They were a bargain!

A bargain, you say?
Yeah, a great big bargain.

Where'd you get them? I want some, too.
In Filene's Bargain Basement.

In Filene's Bargain Basement?
In Filene's Bargain Basement in their Boston store.

I love them! I love them! How much did they cost?
How much did they cost?
Twenty-seven dollars!

**Twenty-seven dollars! That's the biggest darn bargain
    I ever saw.**
The shoes are great.

The bargain is great.
Go for it.

Lead me to the subway. I'm gonna go for it.

2. Northwest Airlines

Talk It Over

DIRECTIONS: In pairs or groups, discuss the following questions.

1. When you choose an airline for a trip, what things do you consider in making that choice?
2. If you were going to write a radio ad for an airline, what are some of the things you would want to emphasize?

🔊 Pre-Listening Dictation

DIRECTIONS: The following sentences are from the advertisement for Northwest Airlines. After you fill in the blanks with the words or phrases on the tape, or as your teacher reads the sentences to you, discuss the meaning of each sentence.

1. There are two _____ you should ask yourself before you

   _____ a _____ for Asia.

2. Northwest Airlines has good _____ for you on

   _____ _____.

3. For _____, by flying through our Detroit _____,

   you can get to _____ _____ _____ five

   hours faster from cities in the East.

4. It's a shorter, more _____ _____.

NOW GO OVER THE DICTATION AND DISCUSS THE MEANING OF EACH SENTENCE.

🔊 Listen to the Northwest Airlines Ad

Take Notes

DIRECTIONS: You are going to hear the radio advertisement for Northwest Airlines. Take notes on a separate sheet of paper as you listen. Write down main ideas, details, or any words that will help you discuss the ad.

🔊 Listen Again to the Northwest Airlines Ad

Check What You Hear

DIRECTIONS: Rewind the tape and listen again to the ad for Northwest Airlines. Following are sentences from the tape in the order that you will hear them. There are also some sentences that are not on the tape. Listen carefully, and when you hear one of the sentences, put a check (✓) beside it.

1. ___ Before you book a flight for Asia.

2. ___ Is this the most comfortable way to get there?

3. ___ You can get to Asia up to five hours faster.

4. ___ Fly from beautiful California.

5. ___ The connection is quick and convenient.

6. ___ There's more personal space.

7. ___ The food is delicious.

8. ___ [You have] your own personal video system.

9. ___ Call your travel agent.

10. ___ Some people just know how to fly.

DISCUSS THE MEANING OF EACH SENTENCE. THEN GO BACK AND LISTEN AGAIN TO THE AD FOR NORTHWEST AIRLINES.

Check Your Understanding

True or False

DIRECTIONS: Decide whether the following seven phrases used to complete the sentence are true or false according to the information you have heard in the ad for Northwest Airlines. Mark T (for true) or F (for false) for each phrase.

According to the advertisement, there are advantages for getting to Asia on Northwest Airlines from the United States if you

1. ___ live in New York City.

2. ___ live in Los Angeles.

3. ___ live in Miami.

4. ___ enjoy classical music.

5. ___ need more space for sleeping.

6. ___ want to save a lot of money.

7. ___ want the best airline food.

Recycling Key Vocabulary

DIRECTIONS: In pairs or groups, explain the meaning of the underlined word(s) in each sentence (a), then explain the meaning of the entire sentence in the context of the ad for Northwest Airlines. Then answer the follow-up question (b).

1. **Book a flight**

   a. There are two things you should ask yourself before you book a flight for Asia.

   b. Give details about the last time you booked a flight: where, when, for what destination, seat location, and so on.

2. **Business Class**

   a. Travel in the comfort of Northwest Business Class.

   b. Tell what you know about different "classes" on airlines. What are the differences among them?

Questions for Discussion

1. List the selling points of Northwest Airlines that are given in the ad.
2. Evaluate the ad. Is it convincing? Why or why not?

📼 Short Conversation

DIRECTIONS: Listen to the short conversation on tape, then answer each of the five follow-up questions by circling the letter of the correct answer below.

1. **a.** his brother in Seattle

   b. a bus station

   c. information about arrivals

   d. an airline

2. **a.** He was too busy to call.

   b. He needed to speak to the manager.

c. All the lines were busy.

d. The woman didn't want to talk with him.

3. **a.** His brother is getting married.

   b. He is getting married.

   c. He has an interview for a job.

   d. He can get there any day.

4. **a.** He is very organized.

   b. He does not think ahead.

   c. He is very efficient.

   d. He expects the worst.

5. **a.** He will try to get a direct route.

   b. He will try to fly on the twenty-fifth.

   c. He will try to fly on the twenty-third.

   d. He will stay in Boston.

CHAPTER 7

Labor Day Jim, Postal Carrier

Do you think that you would like a job with the post office? Jim, who is a postal carrier, explains why this work is a labor of love for him.

🔊 Introduction

Labor Day in the United States is a national holiday that is celebrated on the first Monday in September. The creators of the holiday wanted to honor the contributions that workers have made to the strength, prosperity, and well-being of the country. The first Labor Day was celebrated on September 5, 1882, in New York City. Twelve years later, the U.S. Congress passed an act making Labor Day a legal holiday in all of the United States.

One recent Labor Day, WRKO—a talk station in Boston—had a special program about workers. The host of the program, Steve Weisman, asked listeners to call the station and talk about their jobs. He asked them to answer these questions: Why did you go into your job? Are you happy or unhappy with your job? Why? Is your job stressful? Why or why not? What do you think would be the best job in the world? The worst job?

One of the callers that afternoon was a man named Jim, who works for the U.S. Postal Service as a mail carrier. What does Jim say about his job? Does he like it or not? Why? What else does he talk about?

Talk It Over

DIRECTIONS: In pairs or groups, discuss the following questions.

1. Have you ever worked?
2. What kind of a job did you have?
3. What did you enjoy or *not* enjoy about your job?
4. Did that job ever cause you stress?
5. What do you think is the best job in the world?
6. What do you think is the worst job in the world?

🔊 First Pre-Listening Dictation

DIRECTIONS: The following sentences are from the conversation between radio host Steve Weisman and Jim. After you fill in the blanks with the words or phrases on the tape, or as your teacher reads the sentences to you, discuss the meaning of each sentence.

1. I don't like being _____ _____.

2. We don't have _____ looking over _____ _____

_____.

3. Everybody's on . . . a _____-_____ basis.

4. There's _____ a lot of _____ there.

5. And you _____ complain a lot.

6. Then it's really an _____ job.

7. A traveling _____ taster, where everything's a junket.

8. Something about _____ out sewers.

9. Did she start lingering and happen to be _____ there?

10. Hadn't it been for a _____, of walking around the neighbor-

hood on a Sunday, we _____ have _____.

11. _____ not as much animosity.

12. The _____ is _____ and foremost.

**NOW GO OVER THE DICTATION AND DISCUSS THE MEANING OF EACH
SENTENCE.**

Second Pre-Listening Dictation

DIRECTIONS: These sentences also are from the conversation with Jim. After
you fill in the blanks with the missing words or phrases as your teacher reads
the sentences to you, repeat them aloud. If you have the opportunity, record
them on a blank tape.

1. I don't like being _____ up.

2. We don't have _____ looking over our _____.

3. Everybody's _____ . . . a _____-_____

basis.

4. There's not a lot of _____ there.

5. There's not as much _____.

6. The _____ is _____ and _____.

NOW REPEAT THE SENTENCES ALOUD.

🔊 Listen to "Labor Day"

Take Notes

DIRECTIONS: You are going to hear the conversation between radio host Steve Weisman and Jim. Take notes on a separate sheet of paper as you listen. Write down main ideas, details, or any words that will help you discuss the conversation.

🔊 Listen Again to "Labor Day"

Check What You Hear

DIRECTIONS: Rewind the tape and listen again to the conversation with Jim. Following are sentences from the tape in the order that you will hear them. There are also some sentences that are not on the tape. Listen carefully, and when you hear one of the sentences, put a check (✓) beside it.

1. ___ I am a postal worker and a mail carrier.

2. ___ The carriers are the best job.

3. ___ We're out there on the street.

4. ___ I can wear short trousers on my job.

5. ___ You don't have those supervisors with you all that time.

6. ___ That sounds pretty good.

7. ___ Something about cleaning out sewers.

8. ___ Do you . . . like it a little less when those windy, wintry, snowy days come?

9. ___ You get used to it, to tell you the truth.

10. ___ I hate it when the snow is deep.

11. ___ If I could just add a little interdiction here.

12. ___ I'd like my job better if I lived in Florida.

13. ___ I'll always be her mail carrier.

14. ___ There's none of that kind of stress.

15. ___ The attitude is first and foremost.

DISCUSS THE MEANING OF EACH SENTENCE. THEN GO BACK AND LISTEN AGAIN TO THE CONVERSATION WITH JIM.

Check Your Understanding

📼 True or False

DIRECTIONS: You will hear ten sentences on tape. Decide whether the sentences are true or false according to the information you have heard in the conversation with Jim. Mark T (for true) or F (for false) for each sentence.

1. ___ 2. ___ 3. ___ 4. ___ 5. ___ 6. ___ 7. ___ 8. ___ 9. ___ 10. ___

Recycling the Information

DIRECTIONS: Underline the word or phrase in each set of brackets that gives the correct information according to the conversation with Jim.

Jim says that one of the reasons he [likes, dislikes] his job at the post office is that during a regular day there, he works [only indoors, only outdoors, both indoors and outdoors]. He reports that he has a supervisor [all day, part of the day, only one day each week]. He works in a small station where the people are quite [formal, informal] with each other, so when they talk with each other, they use their [first, last, middle] names.

He thinks that it would be wonderful to have a job as someone who [tastes, prepares, sells] food.

He is married. He met his wife one day when he was [delivering mail, working in the post office, walking in the neighborhood]. When Steve Weisman asks him if he delivers mail at her house these days, he says no, but he will always be her [husband, lover, mail carrier].

It is generally believed that postal workers have [very little, some, much] stress in their work. Jim says that in regard to stress, his post office is not typical because it is [small, large, medium] in size and the workers there are [friendly, angry, frustrated] with each other.

He thinks that it is very important for workers in any job to have [self-respect, respect for the supervisor, a good education]. Most important of all, he says, a worker anywhere needs to have [enough sleep each night, a positive feeling about the job, a good family life].

Recycling Key Vocabulary

DIRECTIONS: In pairs or groups, explain the meaning of the underlined word(s) in each sentence (a), then explain the meaning of the entire sentence in the context of the conversation with Jim. Then answer the follow-up question (b).

1. **To be cooped up**

   a. I don't like being cooped up.

   b. Tell about a time when you felt cooped up.

2. **To complain**

   a. You do it well, and you don't complain a lot.

   b. What kinds of things do you sometimes complain about?

3. **Easygoing**

   a. Then it's really an easygoing job, and I do like it.

   b. Do people think that you are an easygoing person? Explain.

4. **Roughly**

   a. Her job hours are roughly the same as mine.

   b. Roughly speaking, how long have you studied English?

5. **Stress**

   a. Where I am in, there's none of that kind of stress.

   b. Under what circumstances do you feel stress?

6. **First and foremost**

   a. The attitude is first and foremost.

   b. What is first and foremost in your life at the present time?

Questions for Discussion

1. Why do you think people who work in the post office feel more stress than people who deliver the mail?

2. What are Jim's ideas about the best job and the worst job in the world?

3. Why does Jim like his job?

4. Explain how Jim met his wife.

📼 Short Conversation

DIRECTIONS: Listen to the short conversation on tape, then answer each of the three follow-up questions by circling the letter of the correct answer below.

1. **a.** at an employment agency

   b. in the newspaper

   c. over the Internet

   d. at his friend's factory

2. **a.** that there is no stress

   b. that there is no heavy work

   c. that he can work outdoors

   d. that he doesn't have to travel a long way

3. **a.** He thinks it's a good thing.

   b. He would like to be a supervisor.

   c. He doesn't like it.

   d. He thinks it's necessary.

Former President Jimmy Carter Jimmy Carter, Poet

The thirty-ninth president of the United States reads and explains one of his quite personal poems.

📼 Introduction

James Earl "Jimmy" Carter, Jr., was president of the United States from 1977 to 1981. Since that time, he has been very active in a variety of pursuits, and some people say that he is the best former president this country has ever had.

Carter and his wife, Rosalynn, have worked for several years with Habitat for Humanity, an organization of thousands of volunteers who build houses for—and with—people who need them but can't afford all the building expenses.

After he created the Carter Center in Atlanta, Georgia, in 1986, he became very active as a global peacemaker. He and other members of the center have been invited to many countries—including North Korea, Haiti, Bosnia, and Nicaragua—to help them resolve conflicts with their neighbors or enemies within the country. In his role as peacemaker, he has served as an independent observer of elections in various countries.

In addition to his humanitarian activities, Carter has long enjoyed writing poetry. He gathered some of his favorite poems together in a book titled *Always a Reckoning*, which was published in 1994. Here, from that book, is a poem that you will hear him read on tape.

Difficult Times

I try to understand.
I've seen you draw away
and show the pain.
It's hard to know what I can say
to turn things right again,
to have the coolness melt,
to share once more
the warmth we've felt.

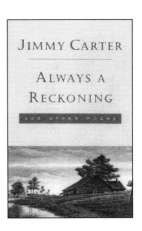

Talk It Over

DIRECTIONS: In pairs or groups, discuss the following questions.

1. Who do you think is the "I" in this poem? Who is the "you" ?
2. What are some possible sources of the "pain"?
3. Do you like poetry? Have you ever written a poem?
4. Did you study a lot of poetry in school?
5. Did you have to memorize a lot of poetry in school? How many poems (or parts of poems) can you remember?

🔊 First Pre-Listening Dictation

DIRECTIONS: The following sentences are from Terry Gross's interview with Jimmy Carter. After you fill in the blanks with the words or phrases on the tape, or as your teacher reads the sentences to you, discuss the meaning of each sentence.

1. I _____ it several times to _____ it and abbreviate it.

2. But I think we all go _____ those _____.

3. Did that help . . . _____ things _____?

4. This is an _____ of a _____ that I would expect you _____ have reservations publishing if you were in the _____ _____.

5. What was the _____ about, and how long _____ it last?

6. They are too _____-revealing, and they open up questions.

7. You know, five years _____ and _____.

NOW GO OVER THE DICTATION AND DISCUSS THE MEANING OF EACH SENTENCE.

Second Pre-Listening Dictation

DIRECTIONS: These sentences also are from the interview with Jimmy Carter. After you fill in the blanks with the missing words or phrases as your teacher reads the sentences to you, repeat them aloud. If you have the opportunity, record them on a blank tape.

1. But I think we all go _____ those _____.

2. Did that help . . . _____ things _____?

3. I would expect you might have _____.

4. How long _____ _____ _____?

5. You know, for five years, _____ and _____.

NOW REPEAT THE SENTENCES ALOUD.

Listen to Former President Carter

Take Notes

DIRECTIONS: You are going to hear Terry Gross's interview with Jimmy Carter. Take notes on a separate sheet of paper as you listen. Write down main ideas, details, or any words that will help you discuss the interview.

Listen Again to Former President Carter

Check What You Hear

DIRECTIONS: Rewind the tape and listen again to the interview with Jimmy Carter. Following are sentences from the tape in the order that you will hear them. There are also some sentences that are not on the tape. Listen carefully, and when you hear one of the sentences, put a check (✓) beside it.

1. ___ I try to understand.

2. ___ Yes, when we were having some difficult times.

3. ___ I rewrote it several times to simplify it and abbreviate it.

4. ___ I wrote five versions.

5. ___ There's a reaching out to someone else that can be expressed in poetry.

6. ___ What was the dispute about, and how long did it last?

7. ___ My wife didn't like the poem at first.

8. ___ I can kind of be evasive if I want.

9. ___ You're a very good interviewer.

10. ___ These poems took a lot of work.

11. ___ People don't understand how much work is involved.

12. ___ They're a product of a great deal of self-examination.

DISCUSS THE MEANING OF EACH SENTENCE. THEN GO BACK AND LISTEN AGAIN TO THE INTERVIEW WITH JIMMY CARTER.

Check Your Understanding

True or False

DIRECTIONS: You will hear eight sentences on tape. Decide whether the sentences are true or false according to the information you have heard in the interview with Jimmy Carter. Mark T (for true) or F (for false) for each sentence.

1. ___   2. ___   3. ___   4. ___   5. ___   6. ___   7. ___   8. ___

Recycling the Information

DIRECTIONS: Underline the word or phrase in each set of brackets that gives the correct information according to the interview with Jimmy Carter.

In this interview, Jimmy Carter reads a short poem that he wrote. The poem tells about the [joy, sadness, anger] he felt at a time when he and his wife were having [a vacation, a problem, their anniversary celebration]. The poem tells about his [difficulty, ease, fun] in finding the right [words, gift, book] to [buy, send, say].

He explains to the interviewer that he [wrote, published, erased] the poems [before, while, after] he was president because he thought that perhaps [newspaper writers, Rosalynn, his mother] might ask him [easy, funny, personal] questions that he [would, would not] want to answer if he was [still president, not president, married to Rosalynn].

Carter says that he couldn't write poems while he was in the White House because he [didn't have time, wasn't interested, was afraid of the press]. From what he says, we know that in most of his poems, he is writing about [his presidency, being a peacemaker, his thoughts and feelings].

Recycling Key Vocabulary

DIRECTIONS: In pairs or groups, explain the meaning of the underlined word(s) in each sentence (a), then explain the meaning of the entire sentence in the context of the interview with Jimmy Carter. Then answer the follow-up question (b).

1. **To go through**

   a. We all go through those things.

   b. Tell about a difficult experience you have recently gone through.

2. **Reservations**

   a. I would expect you might have reservations.

   b. People sometimes have reservations about getting married. Do you agree with this statement? Explain. Also, what is another meaning of the word *reservation(s)*?

3. **Dispute**

   a. What was the dispute about?

   b. Tell about a dispute you have had with someone.

4. **A great deal**

    a. They're a product of <u>a great deal</u> of self-examination.

    b. What are some activities on which you spend a great deal of time?

Questions for Discussion

1. Jimmy Carter explains why he wrote this poem. What does he say?
2. The former president says that he would not have published his poems while he was living in the White House. Why?
3. Does he think that writing poetry is easy or difficult? Explain.

Suggested Activity

DIRECTIONS: Find a poem in your native language that you like. Bring it to class and share it with your classmates, telling them in English what the poem is about and possibly giving them some information about the poet.

Lecture

DIRECTIONS: Listen to the short lecture on tape, then answer each of the four follow-up questions by circling the letter of the correct answer below.

1. **a.** "Rhymes and Games"

    b. "Nursery Rhymes"

    c. "Where Nursery Rhymes Were Written"

    d. "Children's Games"

2. **a.** They were all written by adults.

    b. They were written by professional writers.

    c. They were all created in Europe and China.

    d. They were probably made up by both children and adults.

3. **a.** Nursery rhymes are very old.

    b. Nursery rhymes began in this century.

c. Nursery rhymes are always about animals.

d. Nursery rhymes began in the nineteenth century.

4. a. They can be sung.

b. They are very short.

c. They are easy to memorize.

d. They are a good introduction to poetry.

English Nursery Rhymes

DIRECTIONS: The following nursery rhymes are missing several words. Use the list of words to fill in the blanks. (Three of these words must be repeated twice.) After you have completed the rhymes, pair off with a partner. Recite one of the rhymes to your partner, along with a nursery rhyme in your language. Then have your partner do the same.

WORD LIST

corner	old	cold	might	old
tonight	I	thumb	pot	hot

Pease porridge hot

Pease porridge _____

Pease porridge in the _____

Nine days _____.

Some like it _____

Some like it _____

Some like it in the pot

Nine days _____.

Star light, star bright

The first star I see _____

I wish I may, I wish I _____

Have the wish I wish _____.

Little Jack Horner

Sat in a _____

Eating his Christmas pie

He stuck in his _____

And pulled out a plum

And cried, "What a good boy am _____."

CHAPTER 9

Parking in Tokyo

A Migraine Headache

You drive around and around looking for a place to park your car. But there are no parking spaces. You think, Oh, why didn't I take the train into the city? You can get a very bad headache if you are trying to find a parking space in Tokyo.

🔊 Introduction

When is the last time you drove a car around and around in a large city trying to find a place to park? And then, if you finally found one, it might have been miles from where you wanted to be. If you decided against parking in that faraway place, you could only hope that you would find a parking garage near your desired destination, but you would probably have to pay an unbelievably high parking fee.

In many North American cities, finding a place to park your car can be a very big headache. In Tokyo, it's more like a migraine headache. Parking is forbidden on ninety-five percent of Tokyo's streets, and because landowners can make a lot more money by building apartments or office buildings, the city has few parking garages.

So what do many drivers do? They look for places where they can park illegally. Not happy about this situation, the government decided to fight back. Under the city's new parking laws, the maximum fine for leaving a car illegally parked overnight is about fourteen hundred dollars. The cheapest fine for a parking infraction runs about seventy-five dollars.

Mr. T. R. Reid, who reports for the *Washington Post* from Tokyo, says that the city's traffic police (cops) are using new high-tech parking meters that send special signals to the police when a car is illegally parked. All things considered, if you live in Tokyo, you think twice about owning a car.

Talk It Over

DIRECTIONS: In pairs or groups, discuss the following questions.

1. Is it difficult to park a car in your city?
2. Do you drive a car? If you do, have you ever received a parking ticket?
3. Describe how one buys a car in your city.
4. Does your city have good, efficient, inexpensive mass transit (buses, subways, and trains)?

📼 First Pre-Listening Dictation

DIRECTIONS: The following sentences are from the interview with T. R. Reid. After you fill in the blanks with the words or phrases on the tape, or as your teacher reads the sentences to you, discuss the meaning of each sentence.

1. When your _____ expires, _____ _____ blink.

2. They see your _____ the minute _____ pulls _____.

3. Your _____ minutes is already _____ away.

4. There _____ some _____ _____ devices.

5. Car _____, car carousels.

6. You _____ need one in _____.

7. I agree _____ the _____.

8. Buying a car is _____ thing _____ _____.

9. Cars are sold _____-to-_____.

10. That's another _____ why car buying is just "_____" now.

11. You've got to have a car or _____ _____ _____.

12. There's _____ place for _____ cars.

NOW GO OVER THE DICTATION AND DISCUSS THE MEANING OF EACH SENTENCE.

Second Pre-Listening Dictation

DIRECTIONS: These sentences also are from the interview with T. R. Reid. After you fill in the blanks with the missing words or phrases as your teacher reads the sentences to you, repeat them aloud. If you have the opportunity, record them on a blank tape.

1. Your sixty minutes is already _____ _____ .

2. You _____ need one.

3. Buying a car is _____ _____ to _____ .

4. Cars are sold _____-to-_____ .

5. That's another _____ why car buying is just
   "_____" now.

NOW REPEAT THE SENTENCES ALOUD.

🔊 Listen to "Parking in Tokyo"

Take Notes

DIRECTIONS: You are going to hear the interview with T. R. Reid. Take notes on a separate sheet of paper as you listen. Write down main ideas, details, or any words that will help you discuss the interview.

🔊 Listen Again to "Parking in Tokyo"

Check What You Hear

DIRECTIONS: Rewind the tape and listen again to the interview with T. R. Reid. Following are sentences from the tape in the order that you will hear them. There are also some sentences that are not on the tape. Listen carefully, and when you hear one of the sentences, put a check (✓) beside it.

1. ___ That's what I think is really diabolical.

2. ____ So you can't feed the meter.

3. ____ And the longer you've been parked illegally, the higher your ticket.

4. ____ I guess people must be then developing real innovative ways to park their cars.

5. ____ There are two policemen on every corner.

6. ____ The tiny little postage stamp where you're allowed to park your car outside your house

7. ____ You can buy a three-level elevator for your home.

8. ____ Some people park their cars inside their house.

9. ____ I've always understood that mass transit in San Francisco is terrible.

10. ____ A lot of it has to do with the way cars are sold.

11. ____ You never go into the dealership.

12. ____ And he does a different block every week or two.

13. ____ *"Myca, myca."* It's the English phrase "my car."

14. ____ Well, it's a pretty big irony that the world's premier automaker is the absolute worst place . . . to have a car.

15. ____ Probably people will stop buying cars.

16. ____ The Japanese auto industry . . . has been trying to build up their domestic market.

DISCUSS THE MEANING OF EACH SENTENCE. THEN GO BACK AND LISTEN AGAIN TO THE INTERVIEW WITH T. R. REID.

Write Five Things

DIRECTIONS: Write (or record on your blank tape) five things you've learned about parking in Tokyo from the interview with T. R. Reid.

1. _____

_____

_____

2. _____

_____

_____

3. _____

_____

_____

4. _____

_____

_____

5. _____

_____

_____

Check Your Understanding

🔊 True or False

DIRECTIONS: You will hear seven sentences on tape. Decide whether the sentences are true or false according to the information you have heard in the interview with T. R. Reid. Mark T (for true) or F (for false) for each sentence.

1. ___   2. ___   3. ___   4. ___   5. ___   6. ___   7. ___

Recycling the Information

DIRECTIONS: Underline the word or phrase in each set of brackets that gives the correct information according to the interview with T. R. Reid.

T. R. Reid is a North American who works in Tokyo. He says that [driving, parking, buying] a car in the city is very difficult. He explains that the city has special parking meters that [see, hear, smell] cars and then send out a [light, noise, odor] if a car is parked for more than [30, 60, 120] minutes, bringing [policemen, other drivers, car salesmen] to the scene.

Many residents of Tokyo buy special [tickets, elevators, permissions] as a solution to the problem of parking at home.

Reid thinks that more people in Tokyo should use [taxis, rental cars, mass transit] instead of [walking, riding a bicycle, owning a car], but he realizes that many people think that owning an automobile is ["in," too expensive, too difficult], so they [go to Hawaii for vacations, install elevators, want a car].

If you bought a car in Tokyo, you would probably buy it from a salesman who [came to your house, sold it to you at the dealership, called you on the telephone]. If you are a young man and you want to be "cool," you need to have a [girlfriend, car, parking place]. If you have *ashikun*, you have a [girlfriend, parking place, car].

According to Reid, the Japanese auto industry has wanted to sell more cars in [Tokyo, all of Japan, other countries], and it has been so [successful, unsuccessful] that now there is [a big problem, *ashikun*].

Recycling Key Vocabulary

DIRECTIONS: In pairs or groups, explain the meaning of the underlined word(s) in each sentence (a), then explain the meaning of the entire sentence in the context of the interview with T. R. Reid. Then answer the follow-up question (b).

1. **To feed the meter**

   a. You can't feed the meter and buy another hour.

   b. How does a person feed a parking meter?

2. **Innovative**

   a. People must be then developing real innovative ways to park.

   b. Describe an innovative way to teach English vocabulary.

3. **Mass transit**

   a. Mass transit in Tokyo . . . is great.

   b. Describe and evaluate the mass transit system in your city.

4. **The thing to do**

   a. Buying a car is the thing to do.

   b. Among your group of friends, what is the thing to do on Saturday night?

5. **Door-to-door**

   a. Cars are sold door-to-door.

   b. Can you think of anything that is usually sold door-to-door?

6. **"In"**

   a. That's another reason why car buying is just "in" now.

   b. Can you think of something that was "in" five years ago but is "out" now?

7. **Cool**

   a. You've got to have a car, or you're not cool.

   b. Describe a cool person, automobile, or movie.

Questions for Discussion

1. If you lived in Tokyo, would you want to buy a car? Why or why not?

2. Summarize what T. R. Reid says about having a car in Tokyo. Use these words, among others, in your answer: parking, high-tech meters, the police, *myca*, door-to-door, cool, "in."

📼 Short Conversations

DIRECTIONS: Listen to the five short conversations on tape, then answer each of the follow-up questions by circling the letter of the correct answer below.

1. **a.** in a car
   b. in a parking garage
   c. at a parking place
   d. in a bus

2. **a.** a parking meter
   b. a parking garage
   c. money
   d. a new car

3. **a.** a salesman
   b. a store
   c. a catalog
   d. her husband

4. **a.** buy a car
   b. buy a house
   c. move to the city
   d. rent a car

5. **a.** A car is necessary.
   b. Parking is difficult.
   c. Renting a car is impossible.
   d. Apartments are very expensive.

📟 Choral Speaking

DIRECTIONS: Listen to the tape and repeat the choral speaking in pairs or groups.

Door-to-Door

Hello, madam, how are you?
I have a remarkable device for you.

What does it do?

It washes the dishes; it sweeps the floor.
I'll sell you one. I'll sell you more.

I barely need one. Why buy more?

It's really cool to own three or four.

It may be "in" to own a few,
but I don't want one. Good-bye to you!

CHAPTER 10

Rosalynn Carter, Former First Lady

Rosalynn Carter, Caregiver

There are times when the people we love become sick—sometimes very sick—and they need us to help take care of them. Former first lady Rosalynn Carter has been there.

🔊 Introduction

Rosalynn Carter has had a very rich and full life. Everyone knows of her role as first lady while her husband, Jimmy Carter, was president of the United States from 1977 to 1981.

Since living in the White House, she has helped build modest houses in various parts of the United States for and with low-income families as an active member of a group called Habitat for Humanity. She also helped establish the Rosalynn Carter Institute for Human Development, which focuses on the caregiving process.

Caregiving has been an important part of her life, and she talks about this in the interview you will hear. What is a caregiver? A caregiver is anyone, professional or nonprofessional, who helps people who are sick or in any way in need of medical or emotional care. For example, doctors and nurses are caregivers; people who look after sick relatives in their homes also are caregivers.

In a book Carter coauthored, titled *Helping Yourself Help Others*, she writes that caregiving has been part of her life since she was a girl. In 1940, when she was fourteen years old, her father was diagnosed with leukemia. He didn't want to stay in a hospital, so her mother took care of him at home until he died the next year. During that time, her mother depended on her to help out in their home and to be a caregiver for her dying father.

Taking care of a sick loved one can radically change a person's life and alter the patterns of family life. In this interview with Terry Gross on *Fresh Air*, Carter tells about her first experience of being a caregiver.

Talk It Over

DIRECTIONS: In pairs or groups, discuss the following questions.

1. Have you known people who needed constant care because they were sick or unable to care for themselves? Who cared for them?

2. In your country who, generally, takes care of people who need constant care? Has this changed in recent years?

3. If you were ill for a long time and needed constant care, who would you want to take care of you? Why? Where would you want to be?

📼 First Pre-Listening Dictation

DIRECTIONS: The following sentences are from Terry Gross's interview with Rosalynn Carter. After you fill in the blanks with the words or phrases on the tape, or as your teacher reads the sentences to you, discuss the meaning of each sentence.

1. We're about to find out what former first lady Rosalynn Carter

   _____ been _____ _____.

2. Taking care of a sick _____ one can _____ change

   your life.

3. In 1940, her father was _____ with leukemia.

4. We were _____.

5. Mother was _____ _____ to take care of him for

   _____ and _____.

6. You just feel _____.

7. And also I had these _____ guilt _____.

NOW GO OVER THE DICTATION AND DISCUSS THE MEANING OF EACH SENTENCE.

Second Pre-Listening Dictation

DIRECTIONS: These sentences also are from the interview with Rosalynn Carter. After you fill in the blanks with the missing words or phrases as your teacher reads the sentences to you, repeat them aloud. If you have the opportunity, record them on a blank tape.

1. We're about to find out what [she] has _____ up

   _____.

2. [It] can radically _____ your _____.

3. We were _____.

4. You just feel _____.

5. I felt really _____.

NOW REPEAT THE SENTENCES ALOUD.

🔊 Listen to Rosalynn Carter

Take Notes

DIRECTIONS: You are going to hear Terry Gross's interview with Rosalynn Carter. Take notes on a separate sheet of paper as you listen. Write down main ideas, details, or any words that will help you discuss the interview.

🔊 Listen Again to Rosalynn Carter

Check What You Hear

DIRECTIONS: Rewind the tape and listen again to the interview with Rosalynn Carter. Following are sentences from the tape in the order that you will hear them. There are also some sentences that are not on the tape. Listen carefully, and when you hear one of the sentences, put a check (✓) beside it.

1. ____ She had coauthored a new book for caregiving.

2. ____ I was the oldest child. I was fourteen. My little sister was four, with two brothers in between.

3. ____ If you are the oldest, you have to do everything.

4. ____ I ate a lot of chocolate when I was a child.

5. ____ My mother is an only child.

6. ____ He was the father figure in our family then for years.

7. ___ My two brothers were very helpful.

8. ___ They washed the dishes and cleaned the floors.

9. ___ Mother depended on me to help her.

10. ___ I had these terrible guilt feelings.

11. ___ If he called me down or punished me

12. ___ But I was a very good child.

13. ___ Maybe they had something to do with it.

14. ___ All these emotions are normal.

DISCUSS THE MEANING OF EACH SENTENCE. THEN GO BACK AND LISTEN AGAIN TO THE INTERVIEW WITH ROSALYNN CARTER.

Check Your Understanding

True or False

DIRECTIONS: You will hear six sentences on tape. Decide whether the sentences are true or false according to the information you have heard in the interview with Rosalynn Carter. Mark T (for true) or F (for false) for each sentence.

1. ___   2. ___   3. ___   4. ___   5. ___   6. ___

Recycling the Information

DIRECTIONS: Underline the word or phrase in each set of brackets that gives the correct information according to the interview with Rosalynn Carter.

For four years, Rosalynn Carter [was a caregiver, lived in the White House, wrote her autobiography]. In her interview, she says that when she was [10, 14, 34] years old, her father became ill with [leukemia, influenza, heart problems]. Because she was the oldest child, her mother

needed her to [earn money, do the cooking and cleaning, help take care of her father].

Her father was ill for about [six months, three months, two years] before he died.

This was a very difficult time for Carter's mother, whose own [father, mother, grandfather] also died. Then Carter's [grandfather, aunt, grandmother] came to live with them for [two, a few, many] years. During those years, Carter had to do a lot of [caregiving, homemaking, work], and she found that she often felt [guilty, sad, happy] and [upset, embarrassed, angry].

She says that she believes it was [bad, normal, good] for her to have these feelings, and she thinks that everyone who has that experience will probably feel [better, worse, the same].

Recycling Key Vocabulary

DIRECTIONS: In pairs or groups, explain the meaning of the underlined word(s) in each sentence (a), then explain the meaning of the entire sentence in the context of the interview with Rosalynn Carter. Then answer the follow-up question (b).

1. **Devastated**

   a. He was sick maybe for about six months. And we were <u>devastated</u>.

   b. Name two events that could devastate you (or an event that did devastate you).

2. **To be tied down**

   a. Mother was <u>tied down</u>.

   b. Can you remember a time when you felt you were tied down? Describe it. Or describe a situation in which you think you would feel tied down.

3. **To take care of**

   a. Mother was tied down to <u>take care of</u> him.

   b. Who took care of you when you were a child?

4. **Caregiver**

   a. Most <u>caregivers</u> are women.

   b. Describe an experience you have had with a caregiver.

5. **To work through**

   a. I was writing my autobiography and <u>working through</u> these things.

   b. When you have a difficult decision to make, how do you work through it?

6. **Normal**

   a. All these emotions are <u>normal</u>.

   b. Do you agree with Carter? Explain.

Questions for Discussion

1. After reading the introduction to the chapter and listening to Rosalynn Carter, what do you think about her?

2. Describe Carter's first experience as a caregiver.

3. What does she say about guilt? Do you agree with her? Why or why not?

DIRECTIONS: Listen to the five short conversations on tape, then answer each of the follow-up questions by circling the letter of the correct answer below.

1. **a.** at home

   b. in the hospital

   c. at her son's house

   d. at a caregiver's home

2. **a.** not to feel guilty

   b. help with his homework

   c. nothing

   d. to help his mother

3. **a.** an airplane ticket

   b. a bus

   c. a car

   d. a ride

4. **a.** a nurse

   b. the father

   c. the daughter

   d. the mother

5. **a.** a nurse

   b. the man's mother

   c. the man's daughter

   d. a doctor

CHAPTER 11

Husbands and Wives

A Caller from Northbridge

A husband tells about what he learned when he suddenly lost his job and found himself at home doing the dishes and the laundry while his wife worked.

🎧 Introduction

Before you listen to this radio show, think about the relationship between husbands and wives as you consider the following married couple: The wife, Mary, does not work outside the home; she and her husband, Peter, have two children, a boy four years old and a girl nine years old. Make a list of all the things that Mary must do during the week so that the home can run smoothly and efficiently.

Peter leaves the house each morning for work at 7:30 A.M., and he returns from work at about 6:00 P.M. Do you think that he should help Mary with any of the housework? Explain your answer. Make a list of all the things that you think Peter *could* do if he and Mary decide that he should help to make the home run smoothly and efficiently.

Now think about this: Peter loses his job. Mary then finds a good job outside the home. Describe one of Peter's typical days after he has become a househusband. What, if anything, do you think he is going to learn?

In general, do you think that is it a good thing for both a husband and wife to work outside the home? Why or why not? Would your answer be the same if the couple had one or more children under the age of five?

When you listen to the tape "Husbands and Wives," you will hear one husband very seriously trying to figure out who does what, why, and how.

Talk It Over

DIRECTIONS: In pairs or groups, discuss the following question.

Who is more likely to have the following responsibilities in your family: your mother or your father (or you or your spouse)?

1. Choose the curtains for the living room
2. Pay the monthly telephone bill
3. Take the children fishing
4. Buy the wine for a special dinner
5. Sew a button on a shirt
6. Take the car to the mechanic
7. Help the children with homework

8. Buy clothes for a five-year-old child

9. Stay at home to wait for the TV repairman

🔊 First Pre-Listening Dictation

DIRECTIONS: The following sentences are from a conversation between radio host Jerry Williams; his guest, Shirley Sloan Fader; and a husband who calls in from Northbridge, Massachusetts. After you fill in the blanks with the words or phrases on the tape, or as your teacher reads the sentences to you, discuss the meaning of each sentence.

1. This is _____ one of _____ days.

2. I will _____, _____ subject my wife to what she's been doing since _____ _____ married for the last _____ years.

3. I was the _____ worker.

4. Two weeks after she _____ a job, I was _____ _____.

5. _____ _____ overwhelming.

6. It's a _____.

7. Everything _____ from bad to _____.

8. It's just one thing _____ _____.

9. It's a _____ trip.

10. I really _____ for granted all the things that were _____ around here.

NOW GO OVER THE DICTATION AND DISCUSS THE MEANING OF EACH SENTENCE.

Second Pre-Listening Dictation

DIRECTIONS: These sentences also are from the conversation about husbands and wives. After you fill in the blanks with the missing words or phrases as your teacher reads the sentences to you, repeat them aloud. If you have the opportunity, record them on a blank tape.

1. This is just _____ _____ those days.

2. It's completely _____.

3. _____ goes _____ bad to worse.

4. It's _____ one thing _____ another.

5. I really took [it] _____ _____.

NOW REPEAT THE SENTENCES ALOUD.

🔊 Listen to "Husbands and Wives"

Take Notes

DIRECTIONS: You are going to hear the conversation between Jerry Williams, Shirley Sloan Fader, and the husband who calls in. Take notes on a separate sheet of paper as you listen. Write down main ideas, details, or any words that will help you discuss the conversation.

🔊 Listen Again to "Husbands and Wives"

Check What You Hear

DIRECTIONS: Rewind the tape and listen again to the conversation about husbands and wives. Following are sentences from the tape in the order that you will hear them. There are also some sentences that are not on the tape. Listen carefully, and when you hear one of the sentences, put a check (✓) beside it.

1. ___ I turn on the radio after I'm done doing my housework.

2. ___ I don't like housework.

3. ___ She was home, you know, due to . . . unemployment.

4. ___ And now I'm sitting in a little office that I had to create in my basement.

5. ___ I'm thirty-four. She's thirty-six.

6. ___ Two teenage girls.

7. ___ It's a handful.

8. ___ And the vacuum cleaner is broken.

9. ___ I only have to waste an hour going to the Laundromat to wash and then come back and dry.

10. ___ She says, "Honey, remember when the washer broke before?"

11. ___ I really underestimated.

12. ___ She was working *and* doing the housework.

13. ___ It just never, ever ends.

14. ___ And that's why they're so stressed.

15. ___ They don't want to rock the boat.

16. ___ They will be better lovers also.

17. ___ They think it's going to be a hassle.

18. ___ They will feel more entitled.

19. ___ He has to put the bread on the table this week.

20. ___ They're more teammates.

DISCUSS THE MEANING OF EACH SENTENCE. THEN GO BACK AND LISTEN AGAIN TO THE CONVERSATION ABOUT HUSBANDS AND WIVES.

Check Your Understanding

🔊 True or False

DIRECTIONS: You will hear nine sentences on tape. Decide whether the sentences are true or false according to the information you have heard in the conversation about husbands and wives. Mark T (for true) or F (for false) for each sentence.

1. ___   2. ___   3. ___   4. ___   5. ___   6. ___   7. ___   8. ___   9. ___

Recycling the Information

DIRECTIONS: Underline the word or phrase in each set of brackets that gives the correct information according to the conversation about husbands and wives.

The man who has called the radio program [has been laid off, is working full-time, doesn't want to work]. These days, his wife is [looking for work, working full-time, working part-time], and when she comes home, she [helps with the housework, washes the clothes, is too tired to talk to him].

The man is now surprised to learn that when he was working full-time, his wife [was quite lazy, watched TV a lot, had a lot of work to do at home]. For example, she [slept a lot, took the children many places in the car, watched game shows]. He now understands that for many years, he [underestimated what she did, didn't like what she did, wanted to work at home].

Shirley Sloan Fader says that she thinks it is a good idea for wives [to work outside the home, to stay at home, to have part-time jobs] because families need [a nonworking mother, two incomes, a nonworking father]. Fader thinks that if both the husband and wife are working outside the home, their marriage will be [stronger, weaker, no different].

Recycling Key Vocabulary

DIRECTIONS: In pairs or groups, explain the meaning of the underlined word(s) in each sentence (a), then explain the meaning of the entire sentence in the context of the conversation about husbands and wives. Then answer the follow-up question (b).

1. **Overwhelming**

   a. All the things that she accomplished . . . completely <u>overwhelming</u>.

   b. Tell about a time when you felt overwhelmed.

2. **Laid off**

   a. After you're <u>laid off</u>, . . . everything goes from bad to worse.

   b. There are many reasons why workers get laid off. Name one or two.

3. **Underestimated**

   a. It's a real trip, and I really <u>underestimated</u>.

   b. What did the husband in this lesson underestimate?

4. **Hassle**

   a. They think it's going to be a <u>hassle</u>.

   b. Do you think it is a hassle to go shopping for clothes?

Questions for Discussion

1. The man from Northbridge says that he underestimated his wife. What does he mean by this? Give details.

2. Describe the daily life of the man after he was laid off.

3. Shirley Sloan Fader talks about women working outside the home. Does she think it is a good idea or a bad idea? What does she say?

🔘 Short Conversation

DIRECTIONS: Listen to the short conversation on tape, then answer each of the five follow-up questions by circling the letter of the correct answer below.

1. **a.** go out for dinner

   b. watch television

   c. go to a movie

   d. be alone

2. **a.** a housewife

   b. a teacher

c. a director

d. a writer

3. **a.** He's been home all day.

   b. He has papers to read.

   c. He's very nervous.

   d. He's feeling overwhelmed.

4. **a.** go to the movies

   b. go to sleep

   c. correct tests and then go to the movies

   d. stay home and grade exams

5. **a.** She is pleased.

   b. We don't know for sure.

   c. She is very angry.

   d. She is disappointed.

🔊 Choral Speaking

DIRECTIONS: Listen to the tape and repeat the choral speaking in pairs or groups.

Overwhelmed

It's just one of those days.
Oh, no. I'm really sorry.

Everything's going from bad to worse.
Oh, no, no! That's really too bad.

It's just one thing after another.
I'm really sorry. I'm sorry to hear it.

I'm completely overwhelmed.
Go back to bed. Tomorrow's another day.

CHAPTER 12

Chucking It All

Mike from Rockford

Do you like to go to the circus? What do you like best—the elephants? The acrobats? The clowns? In this chapter, you will meet Mike, who especially loved watching the clowns—and decided to become one.

📼 Introduction

In Chapter 2, Chris told radio host Robert Siegel what he would do if he could take time off. Here, Mike Hiteman answers the same question. The difference between them is that Mike did more than take time off— he chucked it all, which means that he left his old life behind and started a new one.

Mike was well established in a profession when he realized that if he wanted to be really happy in his work, he would have to make a major change in his life. And that's what he did.

Mike's dramatic move raises many questions about career choices. Is it always best to do work that we enjoy? Should happiness be the major consideration in choosing our work? How important should money be in choosing our work? If we do not enjoy our work, is it still possible for us to be happy and have a good life?

Mike has his own answers to these questions. After listening to his story, you can decide whether you think he was wise or foolish.

Talk It Over

DIRECTIONS: In pairs or groups, discuss the following questions.

1. When asked, many people say that they hate their jobs. Why do you think that people who hate their jobs continue to do them, often for thirty or forty years?
2. If you had a friend who was a dentist and he said that he hated his job and wanted to give it up to become an artist, what advice would you give him?

📼 First Pre-Listening Dictation

DIRECTIONS: The following sentences are from the conversation between radio host Robert Siegel and Mike Hiteman. After you fill in the blanks with the words or phrases on the tape, or as your teacher reads the sentences to you, discuss the meaning of each sentence.

1. _____. Thanks for _____.

2. I _____ juggling and unicycling and that _____ of _____ as a _____.

3. You were _____ juggling two _____?

4. I . . . _____ _____ a contract, performing with the Ringling Brothers [and] Barnum and Bailey Circus.

5. _____, I did.

6. I'm _____ a _____.

7. [Ever] wonder what you'll do when this clown _____ _____ really _____ to you?

NOW GO OVER THE DICTATION AND DISCUSS THE MEANING OF EACH SENTENCE.

Second Pre-Listening Dictation

DIRECTIONS: These sentences also are from the conversation with Mike. After you fill in the blanks with the missing words or phrases as your teacher reads the sentences to you, repeat them aloud. If you have the opportunity, record them on a blank tape.

1. Fabulous. _____ for _____.

2. You were literally _____ two _____?

3. I . . . ultimately landed _____ _____.

4. I'm _____ a ball.

5. [Ever] wonder what _____ _____ when this clown rat race _____ gets to you?

NOW REPEAT THE SENTENCES ALOUD.

📼 Listen to Mike

Take Notes

DIRECTIONS: You are going to hear the conversation between radio host Robert Siegel and Mike. Take notes on a separate sheet of paper as you listen. Write down main ideas, details, or any words that will help you discuss the conversation.

📼 Listen Again to Mike

Check What You Hear

DIRECTIONS: Rewind the tape and listen again to the conversation with Mike. Following are sentences from the tape in the order that you will hear them. There are also some sentences that are not on the tape. Listen carefully, and when you hear one of the sentences, put a check (✓) beside it.

1. ___ And on the line with us now from Rockford, Illinois, is Mike.

2. ___ Was it as a securities analyst or a systems analyst?

3. ___ While I was a computer technician and a telecommunications analyst, I was also a part-time variety entertainer.

4. ___ I liked to read books about bicycles.

5. ___ Which later kind of grew into . . . a part-time gig for me.

6. ___ Four days a week I was juggling and unicycling my way around town.

7. ___ I decided I was most definitely happiest when I was in front of an audience.

8. ___ I was accepted to Clown College.

9. ___ You ran away and joined the circus.

10. ___ Sure. I'm always thinking toward the future.

11. ___ I'm also assistant ringmaster.

12. ___ I don't use computers anymore.

13. ___ I won't go back to corporate America.

14. ___ Unmistakable.

DISCUSS THE MEANING OF EACH SENTENCE. THEN GO BACK AND LISTEN AGAIN TO THE CONVERSATION WITH MIKE.

Write Five Things

DIRECTIONS: Write (or record on your blank tape) five things you've learned about Mike.

1. _____

_____

_____

2. _____

_____

_____

3. _____

_____

_____

4. _____

_____

_____

5. _____

_____

_____

Check Your Understanding

📼 True or False

DIRECTIONS: You will hear seven sentences on tape. Decide whether the sentences are true or false according to the information you have heard in the conversation with Mike. Mark T (for true) or F (for false) for each sentence.

1. ___   2. ___   3. ___   4. ___   5. ___   6. ___   7. ___

Recycling the Information

DIRECTIONS: Underline the word or phrase in each set of brackets that gives the correct information according to the conversation with Mike.

Mike Hiteman, who lives in [Florida, New York, Illinois], made an interesting decision to chuck it all. What he chucked was a job as a systems [salesman, specialist, analyst], which he left to [juggle two jobs at once, join a circus, have a hobby].

After he chucked it all, he went to school for [eight months, eight weeks, two years] to become a(n) [clown, bicyclist, animal trainer]. Now working full-time with the circus, he entertains people with his [Barnum and Bailey, juggling, singing].

When Robert Siegel asked him about his plans, Mike said that he would like to [become a boat captain, return to his work with computers, continue with the circus]. In addition to performing his own act, he also serves as [assistant ringmaster, captain of a ship, a skipper].

If you go to the Ringling Brothers and Barnum and Bailey Circus and you want to see Mike perform, you can look for a [captain, kangaroo, rat race].

Recycling Key Vocabulary

DIRECTIONS: In pairs or groups, explain the meaning of the underlined word(s) in each sentence (a), then explain the meaning of the entire sentence in the context of the conversation with Mike. Then answer the follow-up question (b).

1. **Hobby**

   a. I enjoyed juggling . . . as a <u>hobby</u>.

   b. Do you have a hobby? What is it? How did you get started with it?

2. **To have a ball**

   a. This is my first year on tour, and I'm <u>having a ball</u>.

   b. If you want to have a ball, what do you do?

3. **Rat race**

   a. [Ever] wonder what you'll do when this clown <u>rat race</u> really gets to you?

   b. Describe a time when you felt as if you were in a rat race.

4. **On the side**

   a. I . . . was doing shows on a local level . . . <u>on the side</u>.

   b. In your country, how do people make extra money on the side?

5. **Ultimately**

   a. I . . . <u>ultimately</u> landed a contract.

   b. Ultimately, what do you want to achieve in life?

6. **To land**

   a. I . . . ultimately <u>landed</u> a contract.

   b. What steps did Mike take to land that contract with the circus?

Questions for Discussion

1. How old do you think Mike is? Do you think he is single or married? Is the age of a person and whether he or she is single or married relevant to decisions about career changes?

2. Do you believe that Mike did the right thing?

3. Do people in your country ever make big career changes? Can you think of an example?

Past, Present, and Future

DIRECTIONS: Mike has changed jobs. Using the list of Mike's jobs and activities, put each thing that Mike did in the past in the "Past" column of the following chart. Put what he is doing now in the "Present" column and what he may be doing in the future in the "Future" column. Some of the jobs and activities may fit into more than one column. When you are finished, discuss your chart.

MIKE'S JOBS AND ACTIVITIES

1. working as a systems analyst
2. unicycling
3. working as assistant ringmaster
4. juggling
5. working as a clown
6. going to Clown College
7. working as a telecommunications analyst for a major retailer
8. working as a part-time entertainer
9. landing a contract with the circus
10. working as an announcer or emcee
11. performing his own variety act

PAST	PRESENT	FUTURE
working as a systems analyst		
unicycling	unicycling	unicycling

_____

_____

_____

_____

_____

_____

_____

_____

📼 Lecture

DIRECTIONS: Listen to the short lecture on tape, then answer each of the three follow-up questions by circling the letter of the correct answer below.

1. **a.** You need to study for four years to become a clown.

   b. Many people want to become a clown.

   c. You need to be sixty years old to become a clown.

   d. There were not enough clowns.

2. **a.** juggling

   b. enjoying performing

   c. unicycling

   d. making funny faces

3. **a.** a high school in Florida

   b. a gymnastics teacher

   c. a university

   d. the circus

🔈 Choral Speaking

DIRECTIONS: Listen to the tape and repeat the choral speaking in pairs or groups.

Yes, I Would!

Would you really move to France if you could chuck it all?
I really would move, and I'd move this fall.

So you'd definitely move if you had the chance?
I definitely would, 'cause, I've always loved France.

Is it literally true that you've always loved France?
Just the sound of the word, and I want to dance.
And I'm really quite sure that ultimately,
I'll live in Paree where at last I'll be free!

Oo là là—très gai Paree!

CHAPTER 13

Social Classes

Roseanne, TV Star

Roseanne is one of the great television personalities in the United States. Listen as she talks about her popular television program, her life, and social classes.

📼 Introduction

In the 1990s, Roseanne became one of the most famous women in the United States. Everyone knows her from her very popular television program, *Roseanne,* which ran from 1988 to 1997, and also because of all the newspaper and magazine stories that have been written about her.

Roseanne's successful program was often considered to be the best program on TV. Of special interest to viewers was the program's picture of a working-class family. Roseanne herself grew up in such a family, and many of the ideas for the program came from her own life.

An example of this working-class basis was the show's treatment of money. The characters were always thinking about money and how they could get enough money to pay the bills: rent or mortgage, telephone, electricity, heat, food, clothes, and medicine. In one program, Roseanne takes a job selling magazines over the phone. She tells her husband, "You know what I like about this job, Dan? Nothing." In the show, as in real life, people often take jobs they don't like.

Considered together, the episodes of *Roseanne* provide a dramatic and very funny representation of working-class life in the United States. In the interview, you will hear Terry Gross ask Roseanne if she is still part of the working class. Do you think it is possible to be working-class and also rich and famous? What do you think Roseanne will say about this?

Talk It Over

DIRECTIONS: In pairs or groups, discuss the following questions.

1. All countries have various social classes based on economic, educational, and social factors. For instance, in the United States, we often talk about the upper class, the middle class, and the lower class. The working class is sometimes a fourth category and is somewhere between the middle class and the lower class. What are the social classes in your country?

2. Traditionally in the United States, when a woman got married, she took her husband's last name. Now some women keep their own family name, or the two family names are joined together with a hyphen. When a woman marries in your country, what does she do about her last name?

📟 First Pre-Listening Dictation

DIRECTIONS: The following sentences are from Terry Gross's interview with Roseanne. After you fill in the blanks with the words or phrases on the tape, or as your teacher reads the sentences to you, discuss the meaning of each sentence.

1. How would you _____ _____ what it's about?

2. Well, I mean, when you _____ the kind of money you

    _____, you can _____ _____ be

    _____-_____.

3. That's part of the whole _____ issue that I want to talk

    about.

4. She _____ _____ worry about _____

    ends _____.

5. I was wondering what was _____ it.

NOW GO OVER THE DICTATION AND DISCUSS THE MEANING OF EACH SENTENCE.

Second Pre-Listening Dictation

DIRECTIONS: These sentences also are from the interview with Roseanne. After you fill in the blanks with the missing words or phrases as your teacher reads the sentences to you, repeat them aloud. If you have the opportunity, record them on a blank tape.

1. How _____ you sum _____ up?

2. _____ like to make the _____ of _____

    he makes.

3. You can no longer be _____-_____.

4. Making _____ meet?

5. What was _____ it?

NOW REPEAT THE SENTENCES ALOUD.

🔊 Listen to Roseanne

Take Notes

DIRECTIONS: You are going to hear Terry Gross's interview with Roseanne. Take notes on a separate sheet of paper as you listen. Write down main ideas, details, or any words that will help you discuss the interview.

🔊 Listen Again to Roseanne

Check What You Hear

DIRECTIONS: Rewind the tape and listen again to the interview with Roseanne. Following are sentences from the tape in the order that you will hear them. There are also some sentences that are not on the tape. Listen carefully, and when you hear one of the sentences, put a check (✓) beside it.

1. ___ Well, it's a show about class.

2. ___ It's about the middle class.

3. ___ Your life has gotten further and further away from the life of the Roseanne character.

4. ___ Does working-class *just* mean how much money you make?

5. ___ I think it does.

6. ___ It is a culture.

7. ___ I have a big mortgage and a big house.

8. ___ Do you understand what I'm saying?

9. ___ Rich people are just like you and me.

10. ___ That's just totally ridiculous.

11. ___ I'm wondering why you decided to change your name.

12. ___ A lot of women don't do it in general anymore.

13. ___ I wanted that period of my life to be over.

14. ___ I joined a new family.

DISCUSS THE MEANING OF EACH SENTENCE. THEN GO BACK AND LISTEN AGAIN TO THE INTERVIEW WITH ROSEANNE.

Check Your Understanding

True or False

DIRECTIONS: You will hear six sentences on tape. Decide whether the sentences are true or false according to the information you have heard in the interview with Roseanne. Mark T (for true) or F (for false) for each sentence.

1. ___   2. ___   3. ___   4. ___   5. ___   6. ___

Recycling the Information

DIRECTIONS: Underline the word or phrase in each set of brackets that gives the correct information according to the interview with Roseanne.

Roseanne has become famous as a result of her very popular [television show, movie, theatrical production]. In addition, Roseanne has recently written [her autobiography, a television series, a book of poetry]. Asked by Terry Gross to sum up her TV program, Roseanne says that it is about [money, family, class] and also about [women, happiness, men]. Gross points out that now that Roseanne has become very [upper class, rich, unhappy], it must be very difficult to be the star of a program about [working-class, middle-class, wealthy] people.

Roseanne [agrees, disagrees] with her, saying that she believes that she will always be [upper-, middle-, working-] class, even though she is [rich, unhappy, poor], because she lived so much of her life [married, in the working class, in business].

During the interview, it is clear that Gross thinks that Roseanne no longer has problems with [family, money, health]. Roseanne, who becomes a little [pleased, sad, angry], explains that her life is [like, unlike] the lives of other people because she [does, doesn't] need to worry about [work, her family, her husband].

Finally, Gross asks her about her [daughter, mother, name]. Roseanne says that she now has her [father's, mother's, husband's] name because, for one thing, she [loves, doesn't like, doesn't see] her father.

Recycling Key Vocabulary

DIRECTIONS: In pairs or groups, explain the meaning of the underlined word(s) in each sentence (a), then explain the meaning of the entire sentence in the context of the interview with Roseanne. Then answer the follow-up question (b).

1. **To sum up**

   a. How would you sum up what it's about?

   b. Sum up what you think about life in the United States.

2. **Class**

   a. Well, it's a show about class.

   b. Describe a working-class or an upper-class family in your country.

3. **To make money**

   a. Does working-class just mean how much money you make?

   b. How do you plan to make money in the future?

4. **Culture**

   a. That is the <u>culture</u> I was raised in.

   b. What do you think is the most difficult thing about adapting to a new culture?

Questions for Discussion

1. Do you think that this interview was easy or difficult for Terry Gross? Explain your answer.
2. Do you think that you would like to meet Roseanne? Why or why not?
3. What do you think about her remarks about her father?
4. What do you think about Roseanne's ideas about social class?

🔘 Lecture

DIRECTIONS: Listen to the short lecture on tape, then answer each of the five follow-up questions by circling the letter of the correct answer below.

1. **a.** "Warner's Six Social Classes"

   b. "A Classless Society"

   c. "Social Classes"

   d. "The Middle Class"

2. **a.** It is based on education.

   b. It is based on ancestry.

   c. It is informal.

   d. It is classless.

3. **a.** a social studies teacher

   b. a professor at New York University

   c. unknown

   d. a social anthropologist

4. **a.** sixteen

   b. sixty

    c. six

    d. three

5. **a.** People can move between social classes.

    b. People won't move between social classes.

    c. People don't move between social classes.

    d. People can't move between social classes.

CHAPTER 14

A Life-Changing Event

Brent Staples, Editorial Writer

Is it possible that a short conversation with a stranger can completely change a person's life? Brent Staples thinks so.

🔊 Introduction

Perhaps you know someone who has said something like this to you: "There is one major experience in my life that changed everything for me. If you ask me who I am, what my work is, and why I do it, I will tell you about that life-changing experience."

For example, when Peter Orth was six years old, his father took him to hear Arthur Rubinstein, a famous concert pianist. After the concert, Peter, who had listened to the music with great attention and rapture, told his father, "That's what I'm going to do. I'm going to become a pianist." Today, many years later, Orth tours the United States and Europe, playing piano recitals and concertos with major orchestras.

In the interview you are about to hear, Brent Staples, an editorial writer for the *New York Times,* talks about the event that changed his life. He was a student in high school when he had a short conversation with a stranger. That meeting—a random event, completely unplanned—resulted in his making a major decision about what he was going to do with his life. He was interviewed by Terry Gross on *Fresh Air* at the time his autobiographical book, *Parallel Times: Growing Up in Black and White,* had just been published.

Talk It Over

DIRECTIONS: In pairs or groups, discuss the following questions.

1. Can you think of one special experience (perhaps even a random event) that changed your life or the life of a family member or friend?
2. Do you believe that you have control over your life?
3. Do you believe that luck plays a part in a person's success?

🔊 First Pre-Listening Dictation

DIRECTIONS: The following sentences are from Terry Gross's interview with Brent Staples. After you fill in the blanks with the words or phrases on the tape, or as your teacher reads the sentences to you, discuss the meaning of each sentence.

1. I went to _____ almost as a bolt _____ of _____ blue.

2. I _____ _____ doing much of anything.

3. I was _____ _____ in a local place in Chester, Pennsylvania.

4. He zeroed in on me, and he said, "Are you going to _____ to _____?"

5. It's April; _____ is just down _____ _____.

6. People felt really fairly _____ in doing _____ things.

7. So the thing that _____ was, a man stepped _____ of _____ like the hand of _____.

8. [They] have their _____ made up.

9. Chance and _____ events played a very big _____ in my _____.

NOW GO OVER THE DICTATION AND DISCUSS THE MEANING OF EACH SENTENCE.

Second Pre-Listening Dictation

DIRECTIONS: These sentences also are from the interview with Brent Staples. After you fill in the blanks with the missing words or phrases as your teacher reads the sentences to you, repeat them aloud. If you have the opportunity, record them on a blank tape.

1. I hadn't _____ doing much of _____.

2. I was _____ _____ in a _____ place.

3. Graduation is _____ _____ the road.

4. He does radical _____.

5. They _____ _____ minds made up.

NOW REPEAT THE SENTENCES ALOUD.

🔊 Listen to Brent Staples

Take Notes

DIRECTIONS: You are going to hear Terry Gross's interview with Brent Staples. Take notes on a separate sheet of paper as you listen. Write down main ideas, details, or any words that will help you discuss the interview.

🔊 Listen Again to Brent Staples

Check What You Hear

DIRECTIONS: Rewind the tape and listen again to the interview with Brent Staples. Following are sentences from the tape in the order that you will hear them. There are also some sentences that are not on the tape. Listen carefully, and when you hear one of the sentences, put a check (✓) beside it.

1. ___ I hadn't taken the college boards.

2. ___ I was a middling student.

3. ___ I'll go and work in the shipyard in Chester, Pennsylvania.

4. ___ I also thought about McDonald's or Pizza Hut.

5. ___ The only black professor from the nearby college was in town doing a survey.

6. ___ And he said, "You can be better than that."

7. ___ This is when colleges had felt that initial mission to integrate the schools.

8. ___ Call this man, and tell him I told you to call.

9. ___ I thought this was a very crazy idea.

10. ___ I had to take preparatory math courses in the summer.

11. ___ I stumbled at first.

12. ___ I have been very fortunate.

13. ___ What's the difference between your brother and you?

14. ___ They think it's a matter of constitution.

15. ___ They think it's a matter of sort of basic goodness or Horatio Alger–ness.*

DISCUSS THE MEANING OF EACH SENTENCE. THEN GO BACK AND LISTEN AGAIN TO THE INTERVIEW WITH BRENT STAPLES.

Write Five Things

DIRECTIONS: Write (or record on your blank tape) five things you've learned about Brent Staples and the important random event that changed his life.

1. _____

_____

_____

*Horatio Alger was the author of a series of books written for boys in the early part of the twentieth century. His hero was very poor and had many difficulties, but he always overcame them and became a great success.

2. _____

_____

_____

3. _____

_____

_____

4. _____

_____

_____

5. _____

_____

_____

Check Your Understanding

🔊 True or False

DIRECTIONS: You will hear eight sentences on tape. Decide whether the sentences are true or false according to the information you have heard in the interview with Brent Staples. Mark T (for true) or F (for false) for each sentence.

1. ___   2. ___   3. ___   4. ___   5. ___   6. ___   7. ___   8. ___

Recycling the Information

DIRECTIONS: Underline the word or phrase in each set of brackets that gives the correct information according to the interview with Brent Staples.

In this radio interview, Brent Staples tells about an important event in his life when he was [in elementary school, in high school, working in a shipyard]. This unexpected event, which came to him like a "bolt out of the blue," took place in a [shipyard, school classroom, Chester hangout].

Before this random conversation took place, Staples was planning to [write a play, work in Chester, get married] when he finished high school. After the conversation he had with [a stranger, his girlfriend, the interviewer], he decided to go to college.

He was accepted at a college even though [his grades were bad, he couldn't write well, he hadn't taken the necessary tests]. The summer before he started regular college classes, he took extra classes in [English, mathematics, science]. It was 1969, and at that time, he says, many colleges were looking for students who were [black, interested in Shakespeare plays, radical].

In his first year at college, [he had difficulties, he hated his classes, he lived at home]. Later he [dropped out of school, got excellent grades, lived in a dormitory].

Now sometimes people compare him with his brother. Staples says that he and his brother had [similar, different, wonderful] lives because of [their constitutions, Horatio Alger, one unexpected event].

Because of one random event, Staples decided that he [could be better than he was, should be like his brother, should become very rich]. Now he is working as a journalist for [*Time* magazine, the *Wall Street Journal*, the *New York Times*].

Recycling Key Vocabulary

DIRECTIONS: In pairs or groups, explain the meaning of the underlined word(s) in each sentence (a), then explain the meaning of the entire sentence in the context of the interview with Brent Staples. Then answer the follow-up question (b).

1. **To hang out**

    a. I was hanging out in a local place in Chester.

    b. Describe a place where you like to go to hang out. Why do you go there?

2. **Radical**

   a. People felt really fairly confident in doing <u>radical</u> things.

   b. Tell about someone you know who was or is a radical—that is, someone who did or has done some radical thing(s).

3. **To intercede**

   a. If this man had not <u>interceded</u>, you would not have become an editorial writer.

   b. If two brothers are fighting at home, who will probably intercede?

4. **To make up your mind**

   a. Many of those people . . . have their <u>minds made up</u>.

   b. Do you sometimes have trouble making up your mind? Give an example.

5. **Constitution**

   a. They think it's a matter of <u>constitution</u>.

   b. Describe your own constitution.

Questions for Discussion

1. When the black professor asked Brent Staples, "Are you going to go to college?" Staples said, "No." What two reasons did he give?

2. In 1969, many colleges thought they had a "mission to integrate." Explain what this means. How did this mission help Staples?

3. Explain how the random event of meeting the black professor at the hangout changed Staples's life.

4. Staples explains why his life was different from his brother's. What does he say about this?

5. Staples says, "I have been very fortunate." What does he mean?

🔊 Short Conversations

DIRECTIONS: Listen to the five short conversations on tape, then answer each of the follow-up questions by circling the letter of the correct answer below.

1. **a.** his twenty-fourth birthday

   b. his daughter's birth

   c. his marriage

   d. his daughter's needs

2. **a.** buy a used car

   b. wake up early on Monday

   c. rent a car

   d. buy a new car

3. **a.** He went on a cruise.

   b. He moved to Texas.

   c. He moved to Alaska.

   d. He stayed at home.

4. **a.** when he chucked it all

   b. when he got married

   c. when he got his first job

   d. when he graduated

5. **a.** a life-changing experience

   b. an event

   c. a husband

   d. great difficulties

Answers and Transcripts for the Teacher

Chapter *1* *Car Talk*

FOR THE TEACHER

First Pre-Listening Dictation

1. What's <u>up</u>, <u>man</u>?
2. Hangin' in <u>there</u>. I got a <u>car</u>. I got a <u>brand-new</u> Honda.
3. I started experiencing some <u>engine</u> knocks and some <u>pinging</u> in <u>second</u> gear.
4. It won't <u>handle</u> it going up the <u>hills</u>.
5. . . . until you got to <u>LA</u>.
6. It didn't <u>ping</u>.
7. There's something wrong with the <u>timing</u>.
8. I <u>agree</u> wholeheartedly with my <u>brother</u>.
9. I think your <u>timing</u>'s <u>off</u>.
10. Get <u>it</u> to <u>the</u> dealer.
11. No, it's unlikely you did any <u>damage</u> at <u>three</u> <u>thousand</u> <u>miles</u>.
12. I would tell them the <u>problem</u> and <u>let</u> them figure <u>it</u> <u>out</u>.
13. Good <u>luck</u>.

Second Pre-Listening Dictation

1. What's <u>up</u>, man?
2. I <u>got</u> a <u>brand</u>-new Honda.
3. <u>It's</u> got <u>three</u> thousand miles on it.
4. I <u>was</u> <u>using</u> the cheaper gasoline.
5. It was very <u>weak</u> going up the mountains.
6. <u>Get</u> it to the <u>dealer</u>.
7. Something <u>is</u> definitely wrong.

Listen Again to *Car Talk*

Sentences 2 and 7 are not on the tape.

What Did You Learn about Charlie's Car?

Sentences 5, 6, 7, and 8 should be checked.

True or False

1. Charlie is living in Los Angeles now. (T)
2. Charlie drives a new Honda. (T)
3. Charlie has driven from Los Angeles to New York City. (F)
4. He drove very fast on his trip. (F)
5. Charlie is worried about the pinging of the engine. (T)
6. Click and Clack think Charlie should buy a new car. (F)
7. The Honda has problems climbing hills. (T)
8. Charlie doesn't need to take the Honda back to the dealer. (F)

Recycling the Information

1. Honda Civic, Chicago, Los Angeles, west, in the mountains, the mountain air
2. hear a pinging sound

3. has a real problem, a timing error, see the Honda dealer in Los Angeles

4. take it to the dealer in Los Angeles, agrees with the radio hosts

Short Conversation

Man: Joe's Auto Shop. Joe speaking.

Woman: Can you help me? I have a flat tire on my brand-new Honda.

Man: Where are you?

Woman: I'm on Route 9—about a half mile after the shopping center on the right-hand side.

Man: Hang in there. Someone will be there in about an hour.

Woman: Can you get here sooner? It's dark, I'm freezing, and there's nothing around here.

Questions

1. *Who is she calling?* **(answer: a)**

2. *Where is she probably calling from?* **(answer: b)**

3. *What will she probably do next?* **(answer: d)**

4. *What is wrong with her car?* **(answer: c)**

Greetings, Responses, and Farewells

1. How do you do?	Formal	Hello
2. Hangin' in there.	Informal	I'm fine
3. Nice to meet you.	Formal or Informal	Response to "hello"
4. What's up, man?	Informal	Hello
5. How are you?	Formal or Informal	How are you?
6. How're you doing?	Informal	How are you?
7. Have a nice day.	Formal or Informal	Good-bye
8. Have a good one.	Informal	Good-bye

Transcript

A: Hello. You're on *Car Talk*.

C: Howdy, this is Charlie in Los Angeles.

A: How are you, Charlie? What's up, man?

C: Hangin' in there. I got a car. I got a brand-new Honda. Three thousand miles on it. Just drove it from Chicago.

A: Accord?

C: Yup, an Acc—no, no, no, it's a Civic.

B: Civic. Yeah.

A: So, it's got three thousand miles on it, and you drove it out there from Chicago.

B: You just moved out there from Chicago?

C: Just moved out from Chicago. I took it real easy on the car. The problem is when I got it out here, I—ah—I started experiencing some engine knocks and some pinging in second gear, going up hills. Ah, trouble was, I was using the cheaper gasoline. So someone told me to boost my octane, to go up to the most expensive gas.

A: Did it help a little?

C: It helped a little. It won't handle it going up the hills; otherwise it's fine.

B: Something's wrong.

A: And never had any problem until you got to LA.

C: You see, I had a problem, but the problem was different. The problem was—ah—the—ah—when you get into that mountain the air. OK, well anyways, it was very weak going up the mountains.

A: But it never pinged all the way over.

C: It didn't ping.

A: It didn't ping.

C: It sounded—I was just getting passed by everyone.

A: All right! I can say perhaps the reason you had trouble climbing the hills is the same reason the thing pings. And that is that there's something wrong with the timing. If you were pinging, or if the timing were too advanced, it would even cause you to lose power.

B: I agree wholeheartedly with my brother that I think your timing's off.

C: Get it to the dealer.

A: Despite the fact that it's a brand-new car.

B: Yeah, I'd get it to the dealer and tell them before. Because if the timing is off and you continue to run it with a pinging, you're going to do damage to the engine, and that's not good.

C: Could I have already done damage?

B: No, it's unlikely you did any damage at three thousand miles, but I would have it looked at. It could be something else other than the timing. . . . however I would tell them the problem and let *them* figure it out. That's their job.

C: All right.

A: Good luck. Something is definitely wrong.

C: Thanks for your help.

Chapter *2 Taking Time Off*

First Pre-Listening Dictation

1. You like <u>biking</u>, I assume.
2. You don't think it would be very, very <u>tiring</u> and <u>wearing</u>?
3. It would be a <u>chance</u> to <u>gain</u> some muscle.
4. Yeah, I should <u>say</u>.
5. That doesn't <u>scare</u> you <u>off</u>?
6. I'd <u>be learning</u> while <u>having fun</u>.

Second Pre-Listening Dictation

1. You like biking, <u>I</u> <u>assume</u>.
2. It <u>would</u> be very, very <u>tiring</u> and wearing.
3. I <u>should</u> <u>say</u>.
4. That doesn't <u>scare</u> you <u>off</u>?

Listen Again to Chris

Sentences 3 and 6 are not on the tape.

True or False

1. Chris lives in Chicago. (F)
2. Chris is not a college student. (T)
3. He wants to travel so he can earn a lot of money. (F)
4. He likes to ride his bicycle. (T)
5. He is not interested in learning about other cultures. (F)
6. He would like to make this trip with his father and a friend. (F)
7. Chris wants to travel around the world on his bicycle. (T)

Recycling the Information

1. thirteen, took time off, on several continents
2. develop his body and strength, learn interesting things
3. by himself, encourage others to make a similar trip

Short Conversations

1. **Man:** I really need time off right now!

   Woman: Well, why don't you take it?

   Man: If I do, I won't get paid. I need the money.

   Question: Why won't the man take time off?

   a. He doesn't need a vacation.

   b. He doesn't want time off.

   c. He needs to earn the money.

   d. He wants a new job.

   (answer: c)

2. **Woman:** I'm sorry I can't give you time off this month.

   Man: But my grandmother is sick, and I need to go to California to see her.

   Woman: I'm sorry, Peter. The company has no one to take your place right now.

   Question: Who lives in California?

   a. Peter's boss

   b. Peter's grandmother

   c. Peter

   d. the company

   (answer: b)

3. **Man:** Let's both ask for time off in October.

   Woman: I much prefer July. Why do you want to go in October?

   Man: That's the best time to visit New England.

Question: *When does the man want to take time off?*

a. in the fall

b. July

c. England

d. New England

(answer: a)

4. **Woman:** How long does it take to walk from here to the theater?

   Man: Why don't you take the bus?

   Woman: I'm getting fat. I need the exercise.

   Question: *What will the woman probably do?*

   a. take a bus

   b. run

   c. walk

   d. go to a basketball game

   (answer: c)

5. **Man:** Are you having fun?

   Woman: Yes, you know how I enjoy cooking.

   Man: Good. Please pass me those two eggs and the butter.

   Question: *Where does this conversation probably take place?*

   a. in a theater

   b. in a kitchen

   c. in a store

   d. in a car

   (answer: b)

Transcript

H: Chris, you're on the line, I gather, from La Mesa, California.

C: Yes, I am.

H: Hi.

C: If I were to take time off—I'm actually an eighth-grade student in Montgomery Mills School—I would take time off from school and bike all the way around the world in a chance to see different cultures and get an exposure, to be able to come back where I live and be able to tell people how different—be able to compare all the different cultures to the United States' culture.

H: How would you get across the ocean?

C: Well, I would probably fly across or take a boat across, and then I would travel between the continents on a boat, and then once I got to the land, I would bike or ride across.

H: You like biking, I assume.

C: Yes.

H: You don't think it would be very, very tiring and wearing or it would take a long time?

C: No, as long as I got enough sleep and food and water, I think I'd be pretty much all right. Of course, it would be a chance to gain some muscle.

H: Yeah, I should say, 'cause if you biked all the way around the world—

you're starting out in the eighth grade—it could be time for college by the time you finished this bike trip. It's a long way.

C: Well, yeah.

H: That doesn't scare you off?

C: No, it doesn't, because I'd like—in the process, I'd be learning a lot of things going to different countries. I'd be learning about their cultures, so it wouldn't be just—I'd be learning while having fun.

H: Hear, hear! Would you take anybody along with you?

C: I'd probably want to do it by myself and then tell people about it when I came back.

And then . . .

H: I'm sorry, I missed what you said just a moment ago.

C: And tell people about what it was like and encourage them to do things like that, or if they can, take time off and get a chance to see the rest of the world.

H: Well, of course, that sounds like a great idea, and thank you very much for calling and telling us about it. Thank you.

C: Bye, bye.

H: That was Chris, who's in the eighth grade in La Mesa, California. I'm Robert Siegel, and this is *Talk of the Nation* from National Public Radio.

Chapter *3 The Common Cold*

FOR THE TEACHER

First Pre-Listening Dictation

1. How <u>has</u> this winter <u>been</u> for you <u>so</u> <u>far</u>?
2. I think we tend to <u>push</u> ourselves.
3. <u>Flu</u> and <u>cold</u> viruses are rampant.
4. Everyone around you <u>seems</u> to be coughing and <u>sneezing</u>.
5. Vitamin C . . . does seem to be able to <u>abort</u> many colds.
6. [Vitamin C seems to] <u>shorten</u> the symptoms of many colds.
7. This was very <u>devastating</u> to him.
8. My <u>pleasure</u>.

Second Pre-Listening Dictation

1. How <u>has</u> this winter <u>been</u> for you so far?
2. We <u>tend</u> to push ourselves.
3. <u>Flu</u> and cold <u>viruses</u> are <u>rampant</u>.
4. My <u>pleasure</u>.

Listen Again to Jane Brody

Sentences 4, 8, and 11 are not on the tape.

True or False

1. F   2. T   3. F   4. F   5. F   6. T   7. F

Recycling the Information

1. health, busy, get enough sleep, catch cold, get extra sleep
2. hands, shake hands with someone, hands, eyes, infected

3. drinking, vitamin C, shorten

4. flew on airplanes, pneumonia, take vitamin C, is healthier

Short Conversations

1. **Man:** For me, summer is usually the busiest time of the year.
   Woman: Not me. I manage a ski lodge in the winter.

   Question

   When is the man usually the busiest? **(answer: c)**

2. **Woman:** Don't forget to wash your hands before dinner.
   Man: You're always telling me that.

   Question

   What does the woman want the man to do? **(answer: c)**

3. **Man:** How much sleep do you usually get?
   Woman: About six hours a night. But last night, I slept an extra half hour.

   Question

   How much sleep did the woman get last night? **(answer: a)**

4. **Man:** I don't want to catch a cold or the flu this winter.
   Woman: I suggest you take a lot of vitamin C.

   Question

   What doesn't the man want to catch? **(answer: b)**

5. **Woman:** Let's find another restaurant. This one is too crowded.
   Man: I agree, but I really want to eat Italian food tonight.

   Question

   Why doesn't the woman like the restaurant? **(answer: b)**

6. **Woman:** I hate flying. I'd much rather go by bus or train.
   Man: Let's go by train. It's fine with me.

   Question

   What will they probably do? **(answer: a)**

7. **Woman:** I have all the symptoms of the flu.
   Man: Sorry to hear it. Fortunately, I feel great.

   Question

   What did the woman say? **(answer: c)**

Thank You and Good-bye

1. My pleasure.
2. Thank you, and the same to you.
3. It was no big deal.
4. You're welcome.

Transcript

T: How has this winter been for you so far this year, Jane Brody?

J: Busy, very busy, and I try very hard in the winter to get a little bit of extra sleep. I think we tend to push ourselves. We all tend to push ourselves. There are so many things to do, and there are so many interesting things to keep us up late at night, and then we still have to get up early the next morning to do what we have to do. Um, it wouldn't be a bad idea to try to get in an extra half hour of sleep during this busier time when flu and cold viruses are rampant—um—and you are exposed to all these people who may be carrying organisms.

Well, you know, there was one thing we forgot, Terry, and this is really important, and that is washing your hands.

T: Yeah.

J: Colds are very often spread hand to hand.

T: Um huh.

J: And if you shake somebody's hand, that's the time to wash your hands. It's more important to wash your hands after shaking somebody's hand than after going to the bathroom, I think. So washing your hands and trying to protect—keep your hands off your face, because of course getting the virus on your hands isn't the problem—your hand isn't going to get a cold or flu. It's the fact that you then touch your nose or your eyes. And your eyes, although they're not an infected site, they are a conduit into the nasal passages, so that you can transfer the cold virus to your eye. It gets down into your nasal passages, and you get a cold just simply from having scratched your eye.

T: What do you do when you're in a crowded train, plane, bus, or a movie theater and everyone around you seems to be coughing and sneezing?

J: I keep drinking more and more, and I do indeed under those circumstances—this is another trick I have for flying—is I take vitamin C in a large dose before I fly and another one when I get to where I'm going. Um, vitamin C does not exactly prevent colds. You are—you are just as likely to be infected with or without vitamin C, but it does seem to be able to abort many colds and to shorten the symptoms of many colds. It doesn't work for everybody, and it doesn't work for all colds, but why take the chance if you can get rid of the symptoms fast and fight that thing off? I think that's the better part of valor.

So I take about a thousand milligrams before I fly, and I take another thousand four hours later or when I arrive. And that seems to be helpful to a lot of people. I have a few friends who—in fact the former head of the Federal Aviation Agency had this problem of getting pneumonia whenever he flew on a long trip, and this was very devastating to him, and my advice about drinking liquids, avoiding alcohol and caffeine, and taking vitamin C before and after he flew has really helped him a great deal.

T: Well, Jane Brody, I wish you good health.

J: Thank you, and the same to you, Terry.

T: Thank you, and I want to thank you very much for talking with us.

J: My pleasure.

T: Jane Brody writes the "Personal Health" column for the *New York Times*. Her new book is called *Jane Brody's Cold and Flu Fighter*. This is *Fresh Air*.

Chapter *4 Are You Game?*

FOR THE TEACHER

First Pre-Listening Dictation

1. If you're game . . . give us a call.
2. We'll try to hook you up before the hour is out.
3. Affectionate and honest, daring and pragmatic.
4. Are you on the lookout for our young woman?
5. [It's] getting tougher and tougher every day.
6. I guess people just don't have the trust anymore.
7. Do you know what I mean?

Second Pre-Listening Dictation

1. If you're game . . . give us a call.
2. Are you on the lookout for our young woman?
3. [It's] getting tougher and tougher every day.

Listen Again to "Are You Game?"

Sentences 2, 7, and 11 are not on the tape.

True or False

1. The single white female is looking for an independent man. (T)
2. She enjoys taking long walks. (T)
3. He came to the United States when he was five years old. (F)
4. He has lived in the United States for about thirty years. (F)
5. Tony came to the United States to get a good education. (T)
6. Tony works for his brother. (F)
7. Tony still likes to look for women in bars. (F)

Recycling the Information

1. single, an affectionate, a consultant, thirty-eight
2. Iran, twenty, Virginia, himself, the ideal
3. bars, very busy, her good qualities
4. hard

Tapescript for Personal Ads

Women Seeking Men

Number One. One more try: Attractive, smart, SWF (single white female), twenty-four, with bright smile seeks nice guy to enjoy coffee, ocean, parks, Sundays, music, Boston.

Number Two. Attractive, tall, SWF, twenty-four, black hair, blue eyes, outgoing, sincere, enjoys skiing, outdoor activities. Seeks honest SM, twenty-four to thirty.

Number Three. Asian physician. Very attractive SF, thirty-three, five foot three inches, one hundred ten pounds, loves sports. Seeking professional successful male, thirty to forty.

Number Four. Asian-American TV reporter, one in a million! Seeking professional, successful man of integrity, thirty-nine-plus, thinks big with a big heart.

Number Five. Active, attractive, fit DWF (divorced white female), forty-five, varied interests, including sports, travel, theater, movies. Seeking mate, forty-two to fifty-nine, N/S (nonsmoker).

Number Six. Animals/nature lover wants best friend, DWF, sixty, has owned/studied domestic/zoo animals: horses to tigers.

Men Seeking Women

Number One. True gentleman. DWM, forty-six (look thirty something), five feet eight inches, one hundred seventy pounds, N/S, honest, affectionate. Like animals, dining out, travel, movies, golf. Seek attractive, down-to-earth S/DWF, thirty-three to thirty-nine, for fun, adventure, and travel.

Number Two. SWM, twenty-four, five feet seven inches, athletic, slim, handsome, comfortable, open-minded. Seeks petite SWF, twenty to twenty-six.

Number Three. Asian woman wanted by SWM five feet nine inches. Handsome Omar Sharif look-alike, Italian, fit, great dancer, romantic. Needs F soulmate.

Number Four. Very attractive, honest, stable, professional SWM, forty, six feet, one hundred eighty pounds, physically in good shape, enjoys hiking, racquetball, theater, et cetera. Seeks very attractive SWF, thirty-two to thirty-eight, who is professionally employed, educated, and interested in working on a long-term relationship leading to marriage and a family.

Number Five. DWM, sixty (looks fifty), five feet six inches, seeks DWF, attractive, passionate, warm, kind. Love movies, dining out, and cuddling.

Number Six. Straightforward, sincere, international businessman, athletic with eclectic interests, seeks independent, interesting lady, forty to forty-five.

Transcripts for Personal Ads

Women Seeking Men

1. smart, smile, enjoy, parks
2. black, blue, enjoys, outdoor
3. Very, sports
4. TV, Seeking, big
5. interests, theater, fifty-nine
6. best, animals, horses, tigers

Men Seeking Women

1. caring, honest, travel, golf, attractive
2. handsome
3. wanted, dancer, romantic
4. professional, good shape, interested, family
5. warm, dining
6. international, forty to fifty-five

Transcript

R: I'm going to be reading some personal ads, playing others through the course of the program. If you're game, if the person in the ad sounds like the person you've been looking for, give us a call. We'll try to hook you up before the hour is out. The women seeking men category: Attractive, fit, with long dark hair. Single white female, thirty-one, writer, affectionate and honest, daring and pragmatic. Enjoys eclectic conversations, hiking, bodies of water, film, and blues music. Seeks stable, intelligent, affectionate man twenty-nine to thirty-eight with vital spirit who enjoys work and play, independence and partnership. If you'd like to talk to or meet either one of these people, give us a call. The number is 800-989-8255. The people who submitted those personals are listening this hour.

He's in Tyson's Corner, Virginia—the ultimate edge city. Hi, Tony.

T: Hello, Ray. How are you?

R: I'm OK.

T: Nice talking to you.

R: Well, are you on the lookout for our young woman who submitted the personal ad earlier in the program?

T: Yes, I am.

R: OK. Tell us about yourself.

T: Um—thirty-eight, white, single, five-nine, about a hundred fifty-five pounds, good education, and have my own consulting firm.

R: And Tony, where are you from?

T: Uh, currently?

R: Well, over the long haul.

T: Oh, was born in Iran.

R: Uh huh.

T: Been here for like eighteen or nineteen years.

R: Oh, so you came to get your education.

T: Absolutely.

R: Uh huh.

T: But I came to find the ideal woman.

R: And you're still looking all this time later? OK.

T: Yes, getting tougher and tougher every day.

R: Well, there's a hundred and twenty-five million women in the United States, Tony. I guess it does take a long time to look for just the right one.

T: Where are they—the hundred and twenty-five million?

R: Well, there's a lot of them in Tyson's Corner. It's one of the fastest-growing parts of Virginia.

T: That's true. But you know, like you said, it's getting a little harder to meet people out there. I guess people just don't have the trust anymore.

R: Do you find yourself, Tony, when you're operating your own consulting business—I guess it's not a big staff—you're doing a lot by yourself, you're working so many hours that it is tougher for you to meet people?

T: Uh, that's true. I mean, that's the thing. I mean, you put in a lot of hours in your, you know, company and all that. You barely have time to go out and find someone. And you know, I'm just kind of tired of the, like, bar scene and all that. Go through the same routine, you know. Just want to just pinpoint—find the one you always were looking for.

R: And did anything stick out for you about that ad that made you think, "Hmm, here's a person I'd like to know"?

T: Well, I don't remember the entire description, but I think she was thirty-one, attractive, and I remember some other good qualities.

R: OK.

T: You read the instruction of the male a few times, but the lady just one time, I guess.

R: Well, Tony, thanks a lot for taking a chance, and I guess we'll let you know.

T: Thank you.

R: Bye, bye.

R: Appreciate it. Bye, bye. AYYYIYI. I didn't realize how much people are willing to sort of really put themselves out on the line. It takes a certain amount of confidence to call a national radio program and tell about yourself in a way that's meant to make somebody interested in you. Do you know what I mean? I don't know if I'm self-confident enough to do that. Geez, I mean, am I? Or maybe it's just 'cause I haven't had to think about it in a long enough time that it just doesn't—I'm thinking, this must be hard.

W: It's hard.

R: It is hard. I mean, I'm getting a feeling that I'm right about this one. It is hard.

Chapter *5 Standing on the Moon*

FOR THE TEACHER

First Pre-Listening Dictation

1. I don't think we had any <u>surprises</u> about the actual <u>surface</u> of the moon—about the barrenness.
2. We knew the <u>general</u> configuration of where the craters were <u>supposed</u> to be.
3. You can see <u>ice</u> on the ice caps on the <u>North Pole, and so on</u>.
4. It's just an <u>absolute, incredible</u> view.
5. You know, <u>down there</u> we think <u>it's</u> infinite.
6. <u>It's</u> a <u>shame</u> those folks <u>down there</u> can't get <u>along</u> together.
7. [People have to think about trying] to <u>conserve</u>, to save what <u>limited</u> resources they have.
8. I actually shed a <u>couple</u> of <u>tears</u>.

Second Pre-Listening Dictation

1. We had looked at <u>pictures</u> of our landing site.
2. The <u>sky</u> is totally <u>black</u>.
3. We think it's <u>infinite</u>.
4. We don't <u>worry</u> about resources.
5. I actually <u>shed</u> a couple of <u>tears</u>.

Listen Again to Alan Shepard

Sentences 3 and 7 are not on the tape.

True or False

1. The surface of the moon surprised him. (F)
2. From the moon, the sky looked blue. (F)

3. From the moon, the landmasses are brown. (T)

4. He said that people on earth don't worry enough about the earth's limited resources. (T)

5. He looked down on the earth from the moon. (F)

6. He thought about the earth's problems while standing on the moon. (T)

Recycling the Information

1. fifth, barren, not a surprise, had studied models of the surface

2. brown, black, blue, bigger than, North Pole

3. fragile, be more careful about their resources, the fragile earth

Short Conversations

1. **Man:** What surprised you when you went to New York City?
   Woman: I was surprised that many people were very friendly.
   Man: You know what surprised me? Central Park is so big.

   Question:

   What surprised the woman? **(answer: b)**

2. **Woman:** What was surprising to you at the theater?
   Man: There were so many old people there. I mean *old*.
   Woman: Yes, but they were very enthusiastic.

   Question:

   Where did the man and woman go? **(answer: d)**

3. **Man:** Look up there. It's the earth!
   Woman: Beautiful. But how surprising: The sky is *black!*
   Man: And you can see all the blue oceans and the brown landmasses.

   Question:

   Where did this conversation take place? **(answer: d)**

4. **Woman:** If we go to this movie, I know we'll probably shed a lot of tears.

   Man: Yes, I hear it's very sad.

   Woman: All right, then. I'll bring two extra handkerchiefs.

   ### Question:

   Why will the man and woman probably shed tears? **(answer: b)**

5. **Man:** After we get married, I hope our families will get along together.

   Woman: Why wouldn't they get along?

   Man: Well, you know—small town, big city!

   ### Question:

   What are the man and woman planning to do? **(answer: c)**

Transcript

T: What surprised you most about how the surface of the moon looked?

A: I don't think we had any surprises about the actual surface of the moon—about the barrenness. We had looked at pictures of our landing site taken by previous missions. We had worked with models that were made from those pictures. We knew the general configuration of where the craters were supposed to be. We knew the objective of Cone Crater, which was the one we climbed up the side of to get samples.

There weren't any surprises there. The surprise I had was standing on the surface after we'd been there for a few minutes, having a chance to rest a little bit, and looking up at the earth for the first time—you have to look up because that's where it is. And the sky is totally black, and here you have a planet which is four times the size of the moon as we look at it from the earth, and you also have color. You have a blue ocean(s) and the brown landmasses—the brown continents—and you can see ice on the ice caps on the North Pole, and so on.

It's just an absolute, incredible view, and then you say—ah—hey—um—that looks a little small to me. It looks like it—it does have limits. It's a little fragile. You know, down here we think it's infinite. We don't worry about resources—. um. Up there you're saying, "Gosh, you know, it's a shame those folks down there can't get along together—ah—and think about trying to conserve, to save what limited resources they have." And it's just very emotional. I actually shed a couple of tears looking up at the earth and having those feelings.

Chapter 6 *Two Radio Ads*

FOR THE TEACHER

1. Cellular Phones

First Pre-Listening Dictation

1. The question today is <u>no</u> <u>longer</u> <u>whether</u> to get a cellular <u>phone</u>, but where.
2. An off-the-shelf <u>bargain</u>-basement phone won't look like much of a <u>bargain</u> when <u>you're</u> in need of <u>service</u> and you can't get it.
3. So keep it <u>simple</u> and call Phil DePalma at <u>1-800-695-5400</u>.
4. Right now, get a <u>unit</u> and transportable phone <u>complete</u> with antenna, carrying case, and <u>cigarette</u> lighter adapter for only <u>$29.99</u>, a <u>savings</u> of <u>$50</u> <u>off</u> Phil's everyday price.

Second Pre-Listening Dictation

1. What a <u>bargain</u>.
2. Keep it <u>simple</u>.

Listen Again to the Cellular Phone Ad

Sentences 4 and 8 are not on the tape.

How Well Do You Hear Numbers?

1. twenty-nine ninety-nine
2. fourteen dollars
3. eleven hundred dollars
4. fifty cents off
5. a savings of seventeen dollars

6. Call one–eight hundred–four nine nine–thirty seven hundred
7. Call area code two one two–three six one–two one two one
8. There's a fifty percent discount
9. The speed limit is sixty-five miles an hour
10. For further information, call three six three–two four five five

True or False

1. F   2. T   3. T   4. F   5. T   6. F   7. T

Transcript

The question today is no longer whether to get a cellular phone, but where. And since every place, from your local lumberyard to the corner drugstore, is selling them, it can seem like a difficult decision. Phil DePalma's Cellular Mobile Communications, an authorized Cellular One agent, is the choice. Phil's people don't sell TVs or two-by-fours, but they can give you both the low price you're looking for and the reassurance of knowing you'll be on Cellular One, New England's leading network.

An off-the-shelf bargain-basement phone won't look like much of a bargain when you're in need of service and you can't get it. So keep it simple and call Phil DePalma at 1-800-695-5400. Right now, get a unit and transportable phone complete with antenna, carrying case, and ciga-rette lighter adapter for only $29.99, a savings of $50 off Phil's everyday price. For only about $30 you can now enjoy the safety and convenience of a cellular phone. Great phone. Excellent service. Great price. Phil DePalma's Cellular Mobile Communications at 1-800-695-5400.

2. Northwest Airlines

Pre-Listening Dictation

1. There are two things you should ask yourself before you book a flight for Asia.
2. Northwest Airlines has good news for you on both counts.
3. For starters, by flying through our Detroit hub, you can get to Asia up to five hours faster from cities in the East.
4. It's a shorter, more direct route.

Listen Again to the Northwest Airlines Ad

Sentences 4 and 7 are not on the tape.

True or False

1. T   2. F   3. T   4. F   5. T   6. F   7. F

Short Conversation

Man: Well, at last. I've been waiting on this phone for over ten minutes.

Woman: I'm sorry, sir. This is a holiday season, and all of our lines were busy! What can I do for you?

Man: I need to book a flight from Boston to Seattle leaving on Tuesday, the twenty-fourth, and returning on Friday, the twenty-seventh.

Woman: For starters, sir, what time of day do you want to leave?

Man: I have to leave in the morning. I have an evening appointment in Seattle.

Woman: I'm sorry, sir, but the morning plane is full. This *is* the holiday season, you know. Would you like something in the early afternoon? It will get you to Seattle at six P.M. Seattle time.

Man: No, that's not convenient. In fact, it's impossible. My brother is getting married, and I'm the best man, and I must be at the wedding practice on the twenty-fourth at five o'clock.

Woman: I'm sorry, sir, but—

Man: I know, I know. It's the holiday season. Tell me what's available on the twenty-third.

Questions

1. *Who is the man calling?* **(answer: d)**
2. *Why has he been waiting?* **(answer: c)**
3. *Why must the man get to Seattle at a particular time?* **(answer: a)**
4. *What can you say about this man?* **(answer: b)**
5. *What will he probably do?* **(answer: c)**

Transcript

There are two things you should ask yourself before you book a flight for Asia: Is this the fastest way to get there, and is this the most comfortable way to get there? Northwest Airlines has good news for you on both counts. For starters, by flying through our Detroit hub, you can get to Asia up to five hours faster from cities in the East, Southeast, and Midwest. It's a shorter, more direct route, and the connection is quick and convenient. And when you travel in the comfort of Northwest World Business Class, the flight will seem faster, too. There's more personal space, plus a choice of entertainment on your own personal video system. So for the fastest, most comfortable way to Asia, fly Northwest. Call your travel agent, or Northwest Airlines at 1-800-447-4747. Northwest: Some people just know how to fly.

Chapter *7 Labor Day*

FOR THE TEACHER

First Pre-Listening Dictation

1. I don't like being cooped up.
2. We don't have anybody looking over our shoulders.
3. Everybody's on . . . a first-name basis.
4. There's not a lot of stress there.
5. And you don't complain a lot.
6. Then it's really an easygoing job.
7. A traveling food taster, where everything's a junket.
8. Something about cleaning out sewers
9. Did she start lingering and happen to be around there?
10. Hadn't it been for a fluke, of walking around the neighborhood on a Sunday, we wouldn't have met.
11. There's not as much animosity.
12. The attitude is first and foremost.

Second Pre-Listening Dictation

1. I don't like being cooped up.
2. We don't have anybody looking over our shoulders.
3. Everybody's on . . . a first-name basis.
4. There's not a lot of stress there.
5. There's not as much animosity.
6. The attitude is first and foremost.

Listen Again to "Labor Day"

Sentences 4, 10, and 12 are not on the tape.

True or False

1. Jim works all day in the post office. (F)
2. He doesn't really like his job. (F)
3. He is closely supervised all day. (F)
4. He feels that his job is easygoing. (T)
5. Cleaning out sewers would be a good job, he thinks. (F)
6. He would rather work in cold weather than in hot weather. (T)
7. One Sunday, he first met his future wife while he was delivering mail. (F)
8. In his post office, Jim's coworkers work well together. (T)
9. From what we have heard, we can say that Jim doesn't have a lot of self-respect. (F)
10. Jim has a good attitude toward his work. (T)

Recycling the Information

1. likes, both indoors and outdoors, part of the day, informal, first
2. tastes
3. walking in the neighborhood, mail carrier
4. much, small, friendly
5. self-respect, a positive feeling about the job

Short Conversation

F: What are you doing, Sam?

S: I'm looking through the classified ads in the paper.

F: Do you want to buy something?

S: No, no. I'm looking for another job.

F: What kind of a job do you hope to find?

S: Well, first and foremost, it must be convenient. I'm sick and tired of commuting fifty miles a day. Also, I'd like a job with less stress, and I'm tired of always having a lot of people looking over my shoulder.

F: Good luck. Have you found anything yet?

S: You never know. There might be something here.

Questions

1. Where is Sam looking for help in order to find a new job? **(answer: b)**
2. What is first and foremost for Sam? **(answer: d)**
3. How does he feel about supervision? **(answer: c)**

Transcript

S: Jim in Brighton, you're next on RKO.

J: Hi, Steve. Been listening to you.

S: Thanks. What kind of job do you do?

J: I am a postal worker and a mail carrier.

S: Oh. Do you like it?

J: I do. I like it very much.

S: Do you get—now you said you're a mail carrier—so you get out there.

J: I—yes, every day.

S: Um hum. That part I think I would like 'cause I don't like being cooped up.

J: Yeah, I'm told, from when I got into the Postal Service in the beginning of 1988, that the carriers are the best job.

S: Um hum.

J: Because we're out there on the street, and we don't have anybody looking over our shoulders—

S: That's also—

J: —for a whole eight hours.

S: Yup. You don't have those supervisors with you all that time.

J: We're only in there in the morning. And they're looking over your shoulder. But I work in Allston, and it's a very small station, and everybody's on a name—a first-name—

S: Oh, that's good.

J: —basis, and there's not a lot of stress there. If you want to do your job, you do it, and you do it well, and you don't complain a lot—

S: Um hum.

J: —then it's really an easygoing job, and I do like it.

S: That's good. What do you think the best job would be—ever?

J: The best job of any in the world?

S: Yeah.

J: A food taster!

S: Hah! Yeah!

J: A traveling food taster, where everything's a junket.

S: Um hum.

J: That could be very nice.

S: That sounds pretty good. And how about the worst job?

J: Well, I was just listening to the other phone caller and who said something about cleaning out sewers.

S: Yeah.

J: That's got to be up there—or down there—no pun intended.

S: Now your job, obviously you like the outdoors. Do you feel that you like it a little less when those windy, wintry, snowy days come?

J: You get used to it, to tell you the truth. But the thing is the heat. In the summertime gets me worse because in the winter you can always put more clothes on—

S: That's true.

J: —but in the summer what are you going to do?

S: There's a limit to how much you can take off and still finish your route.

J: And if I could just add a little interdiction here. I married one of my customers.

S: No kidding.

J: Yes. It was one of those stories right out of the fairy tale books.

S: Now let me ask you this. Did she start lingering and happen to be around there around the time that you would come day after day?

J: No, actually. This is odd, but I met her on a Sunday, and as you know, postal—there is no postal service on Sunday, and I met her on a Sunday just walking through the neighborhood where I deliver the mail, having seen other people who I'd known. And I was introduced to her as one of my other customers, and I would have probably never met her because her job hours are roughly the same as mine, so hadn't it been for a fluke, of walking around the neighborhood on a Sunday, we wouldn't have met.

S: That's great.

J: Yeah.

S: And now she gets her mail right on time.

J: No, well, we have moved, so I'm no longer her mail carrier, but I'll always be her mail carrier.

(S laughs.)

J: But I like the job. I know, of course, in the news there's a lot of things about postal workers who go off, and that's always a sad thing to hear.

S: Yeah, let me ask you that—

J: But where I am in, there's none of that kind of stress. I guess that I work in a small office. Everybody knows everybody, and there's not as much animosity.

S: That's almost a cliché about the fired postal workers?

J: That's really one of the reasons why I wanted to make the phone call, to say that I really do like my job.

S: What kind of stress do those people have that all of a sudden turns them off?

J: I really haven't done enough research into the offices where that's happened up there in Michigan, California, and those—I don't really know enough to say. But I can only speak for what I do in my work and the supervisors, they have their job to do, and they do ask a lot of you, but that's their job, and they're getting it from upstairs, too.

But to say something else about how much you like your job—I think that a person who likes himself first of all is able to like his or her job more—

S: Sure.

J: —from self-respect, to begin with. But the person who doesn't like to go to work under any circumstances, they're not going to like their job even if it is the food taster on a junket.

S: You're right. It's the attitude.

J: The attitude is first and foremost.

S: Well, thanks for the call. I really appreciate it. Yeah, bye, bye.

Chapter 8 *Former President Jimmy Carter*

FOR THE TEACHER

First Pre-Listening Dictation

1. I rewrote it several times to simplify it and abbreviate it.
2. But I think we all go through those things.
3. Did that help . . . warm things up?
4. This is an example of a poem that I would expect you might have reservations publishing if you were in the White House.
5. What was the dispute about, and how long did it last?
6. They are too self-revealing, and they open up questions.
7. You know, five years off and on.

Second Pre-Listening Dictation

1. But I think we all go through those things.
2. Did that help . . . warm things up?
3. I would expect you might have reservations.
4. How long did it last?
5. You know, for five years, off and on.

Listen Again to Former President Carter

Sentences 4, 7, and 11 are not on the tape.

True or False

1. Jimmy Carter wrote his poem "Difficult Times" for his wife's birthday. (F)
2. Jimmy Carter says that it was easy to write this short poem. (F)
3. The poem he read was published when he was in the White House. (F)

4. Jimmy says that his poems are often self-revealing. (T)

5. His wife and he often wrote poems for each other. (F)

6. This poem helped Jimmy in his relationship with his wife. (T)

7. The ex-president thinks that Terry Gross, who is interviewing him, is good at her work. (T)

8. Jimmy liked the interview. (T)

Recycling the Information

1. sadness, a problem, difficulty, words, say

2. published, after, newspaper writers, personal, would not, still president

3. didn't have time, his thoughts and feelings

Lecture

Ever since the world was young, children have danced and played games. They have made up songs and rhymed words to go with their game playing. This is as natural for children as their love of fairy tales and music. We do not know how most of these old rhymes began. The children probably made up many and passed them along to other children. Adults may have made up other rhymes.

The rhymes of children cover every subject and game a child is interested in. Some of these things are chasing games, counting games, guessing games, and games that are contests. Other rhymes are about familiar birds and animals, the villages and cities that children know, the bridges they have crossed, and the activities and work that go on around them. Almost everything has been made into rhyme. Children hear the rhymes and change them to fit their country and times.

Children have skipped rope in almost every country in the world and counted the number of skips in rhymes such as this:

> Apple, peach, pumpkin pie.
> How many years before I die?
> One, two, three . . .

The following poem is usually recited to the clapping of hands.

Pease porridge hot
Pease porridge cold
Pease porridge in the pot
Nine days old.
Some like it hot
Some like it cold
Some like it in the pot
Nine days old.

There are many short verses such as this one. Children in every country know short poems like these. Many of these verses are probably as well known as some of the great classics of poetry, and they are a wonderful introduction to poetry for children everywhere.

Questions

1. *What is a good title for this lecture?* **(answer: b)**

2. *What does the lecture say about nursery rhymes?* **(answer: d)**

3. *What is another thing that the speaker says?* **(answer: a)**

4. *Why are nursery rhymes important?* **(answer: d)**

English Nursery Rhymes

Star light, star bright
The first star I see tonight
I wish I may, I wish I might
Have the wish I wish tonight.

Little Jack Horner
Sat in a corner
Eating his Christmas pie
He stuck in his thumb
And pulled out a plum
And cried, "What a good boy am I."

Also see the text for "Pease Porridge Hot" in the lecture.

Transcript

T: There's another poem I'm going to ask you to read, called "Difficult Times."

J: OK. It's a very brief poem. That's the title of it, "Difficult Times."

> I try to understand.
> I've seen you draw away
> and show the pain.
> It's hard to know what I can say
> to turn things right again,
> to have the coolness melt,
> to share once more
> the warmth we've felt.

T: Is that poem to Rosalynn?

J: Yes, when we were having some difficult times. And that first version of the poem is not this one. I rewrote it several times to simplify it and abbreviate it. But I think we all go through those things, and there's a reaching out to someone else that can be expressed in poetry, that couldn't be expressed, at least by me, in prose or verbally.

T: So did you give her the poem after you wrote it?

J: Yes.

T: Did that help—um—warm things up?

J: Well, we're still—

T: You're still together.

J: We're now approaching our forty-ninth wedding anniversary. So yes it did.

T: This is an example of a poem that I would expect you might have reservations publishing if you were in the White House. Because then I could see all the press coming and saying, "Well, what was the dispute about, and how long did it last?"

*(**J** laughs.)*

T: Do you see what I mean? And it just kind of being kind of measured and interpreted in a way that was both very literal and very—very much like the character issue as opposed to a poem.

J: I don't think I could have possibly published these poems, you know, while I was still in the White House. I didn't even try to.

T: And tell me why.

J: They are too self-revealing, and they open up questions that I don't think ought to be explored in a White House press conference. I don't mind exploring them with you because I can kind of be evasive if I want.

*(**J** and **T** both laugh.)*

T: And that's no comment on my skills as an interviewer, right?

J: That's right. You're a very good interviewer, but obviously this is something that couldn't be done. I couldn't have had time to write them when I was in the White House. These poems took a lot of work. You know, five years off and on, of hours and hours and hours of struggling with a line, or with a word, or with a concept—and they're a product of a great deal of self-examination.

T: I want to thank you very much for talking with us.

J: Well, I've enjoyed it. Thank you.

T: Jimmy Carter—recorded in January. His book of poems is called *Always a Reckoning*. More interviews from the archives next week at this time. This is *Fresh Air*.

Chapter *9 Parking in Tokyo*

FOR THE TEACHER

First Pre-Listening Dictation

1. When your <u>time</u> expires, <u>red</u> <u>lights</u> blink.
2. They see your <u>car</u> the minute <u>it</u> pulls <u>in</u>.
3. Your <u>sixty</u> minutes is already <u>ticking</u> away.
4. There <u>are</u> some <u>really</u> <u>remarkable</u> devices.
5. Car <u>elevators</u>, car carousels.
6. You <u>barely</u> need one in <u>Washington</u>.
7. I agree <u>all</u> the <u>way</u>.
8. Buying a car is <u>the</u> thing <u>to</u> <u>do</u>.
9. Cars are sold <u>door-to-door</u>.
10. That's another <u>reason</u> why car buying is just "<u>in</u>" now.
11. You've got to have a car or <u>you're</u> <u>not</u> <u>cool</u>.
12. There's <u>no</u> place for <u>these</u> cars.

Second Pre-Listening Dictation

1. Your sixty minutes is already <u>ticking</u> <u>away</u>.
2. You <u>barely</u> need one.
3. Buying a car is <u>the</u> <u>thing</u> to <u>do</u>.
4. Cars are sold <u>door-to-door</u>.
5. That's another <u>reason</u> why car buying is just "<u>in</u>" now.

Listen Again to "Parking in Tokyo"

Sentences 5, 8, 9, and 15 are not on the tape.

True or False

1. The high-tech parking meters blink when the parking time expires. (T)
2. If you pay more money, you can have extra time on your meter. (F)
3. If you buy a special elevator, you can park two or three cars at your home. (T)
4. Many people use mass transit in Tokyo. (T)
5. Most Japanese people buy their cars at a dealership. (F)
6. It is easy to find a parking place in Tokyo. (F)
7. Mr. Reid says that Japanese women prefer men who have cars. (T)

Recycling the Information

1. parking, see, light, sixty, policemen
2. elevators
3. mass transit, owning a car, "in," want a car
4. who came to your house, car, car
5. all of Japan, successful, a big problem

Short Conversations

1. **Man:** There are no parking places.
   Woman: Should we look for a parking garage?
   Man: No! I'll keep driving and looking and hoping.

   Question:

   Where are the man and the woman? **(answer: a)**

2. **Woman:** Do you have any change for the parking meter?
   Man: Well, I have dimes, but I don't have quarters.
   Woman: That's OK. We can use the dimes.

   Question:

   What does the woman need from the man? **(answer: c)**

3. **Man:** Where did you buy this beautiful rug?

   Woman: Can you believe it? I bought it from a door-to-door salesman.

   Man: Did you let a door-to-door salesman in the house?

   Question:

   From whom did the woman buy the rug? (**answer: a**)

4. **Woman:** After I move to the city next month, do you think I'll need a car?

   Man: A car? That's crazy! The mass transit in this city is excellent.

   Woman: That's what I've heard, but I'm still not sure what to do.

   Question:

   What will the woman do next month? (**answer: c**)

5. **Man:** Look, if you need a car, you can always rent one.

   Woman: Yes, that's true. But I think I really want a car.

   Man: You have to remember that parking in the city is almost impossible.

   Question:

   What does the man think about living in the city? (**answer: b**)

Transcript

Interviewer: In many American cities finding a place to park your car can be a headache; in Tokyo it's more like a migraine. Parking is forbidden on ninety-five percent of Tokyo's streets and because landowners can make a lot more money by building apartments or office buildings, the city has few parking garages. Not surprisingly, most drivers park their cars illegally. The government has decided to fight back. Under the city's new parking laws the maximum fine for leaving a car parked illegally overnight is fourteen hundred dollars. The cheapest fine for a parking infraction runs about seventy-five dollars. T. R. Reid reports for the *Washington Post* from Tokyo. He says the city's traffic cops have even enlisted the help of new high-tech parking meters.

Reid: They [the high-tech parking meters] yell at the cop. When your time expires, red lights blink just to make sure that the parking cop gets over there quickly. They have electric eyes. That's what I think is really diabolical. They have an electric eye. They see your car the minute it pulls in, so the idea of sitting at the meter for a while and doing some work—you can't do that because your sixty minutes is already ticking away.

The meter is smart enough to know if your car has had its allowed sixty minutes, so you can't feed the meter and buy another hour. And it keeps ticking after your time is up so that it tells the cop how long you've been there. And the longer you've been parked illegally, the higher your ticket.

Interviewer: Is there—I mean—I guess people must be then developing real innovative ways to park their cars.

Reid: There are some really remarkable devices designed to fit more than one car into one parking place: car elevators, car carousels.

Interviewer: And these, of course, are businesses. People don't bring them with them, do they?

Reid: You can buy a car elevator for your house, and what they do is they dig down under the one that—the tiny little postage stamp where you're allowed to park your car outside your house—and so there's two levels and then just an elevator, and you can keep two cars in where you used to have only space for one.

Interviewer: Ahh.

Reid: You can buy this for a private home. You can buy a three-level elevator for your home if you've got three cars in the house.

Interviewer: I've always understood that mass transit in Tokyo—and the rest of Japan, for that matter—is great. Why is anybody buying a car living in Tokyo? I wouldn't in New York. You barely need one in Washington.

Reid: Exactly. I agree all the way. You can get anywhere you want in this town. The reason is people can afford it now. It's a new idea. They have the money, and you gotta do something with this money, and you've already taken several trips to Hawaii. You can't quite afford to buy a house yet, and so buying a car is the thing to do. A lot of it has to do with the way cars are sold. You know how cars are sold here?

Interviewer: No.

Reid: You never go into the dealership. There are dealerships, but there is never any human in them. Cars are sold door-to-door. The salesman goes door-to-door, and he does a different block every week or two. And you get to know the salesman over time, and after a while there's sort of an obligation almost to buy from this nice young man. And that's another reason why car buying is just "in" now. You've got to have a car, or you're not cool. As a matter of fact, there's this term that young women use for their date called *ashikun,* which means "Mr. Wheels," and if you don't have a car to drive her around, you can't be her *ashikun,* and that's pretty bad.

Interviewer: This car boom—in fact, I gather there's a name for it even.

Reid: *"Myca, myca."* It's the English phrase "my car."

Interviewer: Well, it's a pretty big irony that the world's premier automaker is the absolute worst place—in fact, an impossible place—to have a car.

Reid: Exactly. And one of the things the Japanese auto industry has been doing, has been trying to build up their domestic market, and they've done it with brilliant success. Of course, they had an incredibly prosperous economy. Now the problem is there's no place for these cars.

Interviewer: T. R. Reid is a *Washington Post* reporter based in Tokyo.

FOR THE TEACHER

First Pre-Listening Dictation

1. We're about to find out what former first lady Rosalynn Carter has been up to.
2. Taking care of a sick loved one can radically change your life.
3. In 1940, her father was diagnosed with leukemia.
4. We were devastated.
5. Mother was tied down to take care of him for years and years.
6. You just feel helpless.
7. And also I had these terrible guilt feelings.

Second Pre-Listening Dictation

1. We're about to find out what [she] has been up to.
2. [It] can radically change your life.
3. We were devastated.
4. You just feel helpless.
5. I felt really guilty.

Listen Again to Rosalynn Carter

Sentences 3, 4, 7, 8, and 12 are not on the tape.

True or False

1. Rosalynn has two brothers and a sister. (T)
2. Rosalynn's father became very sick when she was thirty-four years old. (F)
3. Her father lived to be ninety-five years old. (F)

4. Most caregivers are men, she says. (F)

5. Her sick father never punished her. (F)

6. If you are a caregiver, you probably will feel guilty, she says. (T)

Recycling the Information

1. lived in the White House, fourteen, leukemia, help take care of her father

2. six months

3. mother, grandfather, many, caregiving, guilty, angry

4. normal, the same

Short Conversations

1. **Man:** My mother's at home, and I need to find a caregiver for her.
   Woman: Is she sick?
   Man: She's very sick, and she doesn't want to go to the hospital.

   Question

   Where does the man's mother want to stay? **(answer: a)**

2. **Woman:** My son asked me to help him with his homework.
   Man: Well, did you help him?
   Woman: No, and that's why I feel so guilty.

   Question

   What did the woman's son want? **(answer: b)**

3. **Man:** My friend wants a ride to the airport.
   Woman: Are you going to give it to him?
   Man: I don't have time, but I feel guilty about it.

   Question

   What does the man's friend need? **(answer: d)**

4. **Woman:** I was a caregiver for my father every day when he was sick.

Man: Then why do you feel guilty about him?

Woman: I don't think I helped him enough.

Question

Who was the caregiver? **(answer: c)**

5. **Man:** Doctor, how long must I stay here in the hospital?

   Woman: I think you can leave on Monday.

   Man: Monday? Oh, that's too long. Let me leave tomorrow.

Question

Who is the woman? **(answer: d)**

Transcript

T: We're about to find out what former first lady Rosalynn Carter has been up to. She is personally and professionally involved in the issues surrounding caregiving—taking care of a sick loved one. Rosalynn Carter is the honorary chairperson of the Rosalynn Carter Institute for Human Development, which focuses on the caregiving process. When I spoke with her last fall, she had coauthored a new book for caregivers called *Helping Yourself Help Others*.

Taking care of a sick loved one can radically change your life and alter the patterns of family life. Rosalynn Carter writes that caregiving has been part of her life since she was a girl. In 1940, her father was diagnosed with leukemia. He didn't want to stay in a hospital, so her mother took care of him at home.

R: My mother was thirty-four years old when my father got sick. I was the oldest child. I was fourteen. My little sister was four, with two brothers in between. And my father got sick, and he was sick maybe for about six months. And we were devastated—the whole family was. That's one thing that we learn in studying caregiving is that it affects the family and family relationships. But we were devastated.

And my mother is an only child, and the next year, eleven months later, her mother died, and my grandfather came to live with us. He was the father figure in our family then for years. He lived to be ninety-five years old, so, though in the beginning he was a lot of help, still Mother was tied down to take care of him for years and years and years.

T: What was it like for you to have a sick father at home? Were you responsible for any of his care?

R: Well, of course I tried to help mother. I was the oldest. I was a daughter, and I found out that most caregivers are women. But Mother depended on me to help her, and I knew that he was not going to live, and of course you just feel helpless. I used to read to him, comb his hair, or do anything I could to try to make him happy. And also I had these terrible guilt feelings, because—um—I was only thirteen years old, and as a child I had had sometimes bad feelings about him. If he called me down or punished me or wouldn't let me go across the street to see my friend. *(laughs)*

This was when I was a little girl, a little child. Um, and I felt really guilty—um—thinking maybe if I had been better, he would have lived. I didn't realize until I was writing my autobiography and working through these things that it's normal for children who lose a parent by death or divorce. They feel guilty, like maybe they had something to do with it.

Um, one of the things that I hope this book will do is let caregivers know that it's all right, that it's perfectly normal, to feel guilty, because all caregivers do. Even if they're with someone they're taking care of twenty-four hours a day, they feel that they might do it better, or they feel guilty because they get angry with the loved one they're taking care of. All these emotions are normal, and I think it's very helpful to know that. It helped me to know that it was all right for me to feel guilty.

Chapter *11* *Husbands and Wives*

FOR THE TEACHER

First Pre-Listening Dictation

1. This is <u>just</u> one of <u>those</u> days.
2. I will <u>never</u>, <u>ever</u> subject my wife to what she's been doing since <u>we've</u> <u>been</u> married for the last <u>eight</u> years.
3. I was the <u>sole</u> worker.
4. Two weeks after she <u>started</u> a job, I was <u>laid</u> <u>off</u>.
5. <u>It's</u> <u>completely</u> overwhelming.
6. It's a <u>handful</u>.
7. Everything <u>goes</u> from bad to <u>worse</u>.
8. It's just one thing <u>after</u> <u>another</u>.
9. It's a <u>real</u> trip.
10. I really <u>took</u> for granted all the things that were <u>done</u> around here.

Second Pre-Listening Dictation

1. This is just <u>one</u> <u>of</u> those days.
2. It's completely <u>overwhelming</u>.
3. <u>Everything</u> goes <u>from</u> bad to worse.
4. It's <u>just</u> one thing <u>after</u> another.
5. I really took [it] <u>for</u> <u>granted</u>.

Listen Again to "Husbands and Wives"

Sentences 2, 8, and 16 are not on the tape.

True or False

1. These days, the man is working full-time in a business office. (F)
2. The man and his wife have four children. (F)
3. Their youngest child is in her teens. (T)
4. The man is younger than his wife. (T)
5. They are fortunate that the washer and dryer never break. (F)
6. The man now really appreciates all the work his wife did in the home. (T)
7. We learn something about the sex life of the man and his wife. (T)
8. Shirley thinks a husband should work and a wife should stay at home. (F)
9. Now this man's wife is receiving a paycheck, and he isn't. (T)

Recycling the Information

1. has been laid off, working full-time, helps with the housework
2. had a lot of work to do at home, took the children many places in the car, underestimated what she did
3. work outside the home, two incomes, stronger

Short Conversation

Man: Honey, let's go out tonight. There's a good movie at the Nickelodeon theater that was directed by Mike Leigh.

Woman: You know I'd love to, but I'm exhausted, and I'm completely overwhelmed, and I still have a whole set of examinations to correct tonight. I'm very stressed-out.

Man: Oh, come on. You need a break. It's just two hours. We'll be home by nine o'clock, and you can correct the exams then.

Woman: Oh, honey. I'm sorry. I just don't have the energy to go out for anything.

Man: Well, you know, I've been home all day, and I'm bored stiff. If you don't want to go, I'll go alone. OK?

Woman: You do whatever you want.

Questions

1. What does the man want to do? **(answer: c)**

2. What is the wife's occupation? **((answer: b)**

3. Why does the man want to go out? **(answer: a)**

4. What will the woman probably do? **(answer: d)**

5. How do you think the woman feels at the end? **(answer: b)**

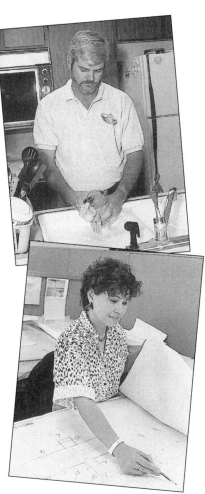

Transcript

J: And now some final calls for Shirley Sloan Fader and "Wait a minute. You can't have it all," she says to working women. Hello.

M: Hi, Jerry.

J: Yes, sir.

M: Jerry, I'm calling from Northbridge, and Shirley, hi, how are you?

S: Hi.

M: This is just one of those days where all day I've been getting what I need. I turn on the radio after I'm done doing my housework, and I got what I needed in the last ten minutes I've listened. I will never, ever subject my wife to what she's been doing since we've been married for the last eight years.

During the last year of our marriage, I was the sole worker. She was home due to, you know, unemployment. Two weeks after she started a job, I was laid off. And I just can't believe it—She would come home and do this and then "Honey, honey—let me do it. Let me do it." And now I'm sitting in a little office that I had to create in my basement with—I just can't believe all the things that she accomplished even when she was just home. It's completely overwhelming.

J: How old are you?

M: I'm thirty-four. She's thirty-six.

J: Children?

M: Two teenage girls.

J: Right.

M: Lucky us. And its a handful. And then, of course, after you're laid off and everything goes from bad to worse, the washing machine breaks. The dryer's fine, so I only have to waste an hour going to the Laundromat to wash and then come back and dry, and you know it's just one thing after another. And I tell her about how my day went after she comes home, and she says, "Honey, remember when the washer broke before, when you were working?" And it's a real trip, and I really underestimated. I don't know if underestimated is the word—I really took for granted all the things that were done around here and—

J: Are you working yourself now?

M: No, this is just it. Two weeks after she got a job, I was laid off, and now I'm home, and I don't know how she got it all done when she was working. She was working *and* doing the housework and the laundry *and* doing this *and* taking the kids here and taking the kids there, and it just never, ever ends.

S: Right. And that's why they are so stressed. And that's why so many people have answered Jerry's questions saying their sex life is nonexistent or we won't ask you.

M: Well, it is right now.

S: Because most men have no idea of how much there is to do, and the women up to now have been afraid—they don't want to rock the boat.

They think it's going to be a hassle, but they haven't felt entitled, and the more they understand that their job is doing for their man, they will feel more entitled.

For example, a man who is laid off, as you are, has the time—when there's another paycheck coming in—he has the time to look for an appropriate job. When a man is the sole support and he has to put the bread on the table this week, men had to take any kind of job they could possibly get, and so her paycheck saves him from that—nicer things. When men come home now and tell their wives about their day, the woman is out there in the world, too. She really can understand. They are more teammates. The marriage has more support going when they are both supporting the family and both taking care of it.

Chapter *12* *Chucking It All*

FOR THE TEACHER

First Pre-Listening Dictation

1. <u>Fabulous</u>. Thanks for <u>asking</u>.
2. I <u>enjoyed</u> juggling and unicycling and that <u>type</u> of <u>thing</u> as a <u>hobby</u>.
3. You were <u>literally</u> juggling two <u>jobs</u>?
4. I . . . <u>ultimately</u> <u>landed</u> a contract performing with the Ringling Brothers [and] Barnum and Bailey Circus.
5. <u>Indeed</u>, I did.
6. I'm <u>having</u> a <u>ball</u>.
7. [Ever] wonder what you'll do when this clown <u>rat</u> <u>race</u> really <u>gets</u> to you?

Second Pre-Listening Dictation

1. Fabulous. <u>Thanks</u> for <u>asking</u>.
2. You were literally <u>juggling</u> two <u>jobs</u>.
3. I . . . ultimately landed <u>a</u> <u>contract</u>.
4. I'm <u>having</u> a ball.
5. [Ever] wonder what <u>you'll</u> <u>do</u> when this clown rat race <u>really</u> gets to you?

Listen Again to Mike

Sentences 4 and 12 are not on the tape.

True or False

1. Mike was a systems analyst before he joined the circus. (T)
2. He was a full-time entertainer while he worked with computers. (F)

3. There was a time when he juggled two jobs. (T)

4. He now performs even though he is nervous in front of an audience. (F)

5. Circus college lasts for one year. (F)

6. He has been performing with the circus for many years. (F)

7. In addition to performing, he is an assistant ringmaster. (T)

8. Mike plans to go back to a job in business eventually. (F)

Recycling the Information

1. Illinois, analyst, join a circus

2. eight weeks, clown, juggling

3. continue with the circus, assistant ringmaster

4. captain

Past, Present, and Future

PAST	PRESENT	FUTURE
working as a systems analyst		
unicycling	unicycling	unicycling
	working as assistant ringmaster	working as assistant ringmaster
juggling	juggling	juggling
working as a part-time entertainer	working as a clown	working as a clown
landing a contract with the circus		working as an announcer or emcee
performing his own variety act		

Lecture

This short lecture is about a very different kind of college in Florida, in the United States.

Would you like to go to a school where you can earn an A for walking on stilts? Or for riding a unicycle or making funny faces?

There is such a wonderful place. It's the clown college of Ringling Brothers Barnum and Bailey circus. In 1968, Irvin Feld, owner of Ringling Brothers Barnum and Bailey Circus, realized that he did not have enough clowns. Clown alley had only fourteen residents and their average age was nearly sixty years old. Feld decided to start clown college to train young clowns.

Clown college is eight weeks of working for fourteen hours a day, six days a week, at the winter home of the Ringling Brothers' circuses in Florida. Classes are held in an arena lined with stilts, unicycles, and equipment for juggling and magic.

Although all of these things are important, the director of the clown college says that what is really important are things you can't teach: sincerity, talent, and a passion to perform before a live audience.

Questions

1. *Why was clown college started?* (**answer: d**)

2. *What is the most important thing in becoming a clown?* (**answer: b**)

3. *Who started this college?* (**answer: d**)

Transcript

R: This is *Talk of the Nation*. I'm Robert Siegel. We're at 800-989-8255. That's 800-989-TALK. And on the line with us now from Rockford, Illinois, is Mike Hiteman. Mike Hiteman. How are you?

M: Fabulous. Thanks for asking.

R: Can you tell me a little bit about first your past as a securities—was it as a securities analyst or a systems analyst?

M: A systems analyst.

R: What'd you do? What did you do with that?

M: I was a computer operations technician and a network telecommunications analyst for a major retailer through their catalog division.

R: Until what?

M: Until I was—I had to make a decision in my life about what I was happiest doing, Robert. And while I was a computer technician and a telecommunications analyst, I was also a part-time variety entertainer. I enjoyed juggling and unicycling and that type of thing as a hobby. Which later kind of grew into kind of a part-time gig for me, where I, you know, was doing shows on a local level as well as doing this computer job on the side. If you're familiar with computer-type jobs, most of those shifts are three-day-a-week jobs, so three days a week I'd be the computer guy, and four days a week I was juggling and unicycling my way around town.

R: You were literally juggling and then, two jobs?

M: Yeah, indeed. And I made a decision at what—I had to determine what I was happiest doing, Robert, and I decided I was most definitely happiest when I was in front of an audience doing my skills and just feeding on the response from them, the applause after the show, people coming up and telling me how much they enjoyed my performances, and I decided that if I could do that every day of my life, that would be indeed the most happiest thing for me.

So I left the computer world and applied for a spot with the Ringling Brothers Barnum and Bailey clown college down in Vitus, Florida. I was accepted to clown college and spent my time during that eight-week program down there training with the Greatest Show on Earth and ultimately landed a contract performing with the Ringling Brothers Barnum and Bailey Circus on this season's tour.

R: You ran away and joined the circus.

M: Indeed, I did.

R: Still with it now? How many years?

M: This is my first year on tour—

R: Mmm hmmm.

M: —and I'm having a ball.

R: And there are no moments when you wonder what you would do when this clown rat race really gets to you, and you've—

M: Sure. I'm always thinking toward the future. There is always life after Ringling, and I'm looking to be performing forever anyplace I can get a gig—either with my clown character, or I'm also assistant ringmaster here in the show. So an announcing job as emcee or per-forming onstage my own variety act or clowning around. I'll continue to do it. I won't go back to the corporate America.

R: Mike, thanks for talking with us. How, by the way, would we recognize you if we saw you at the circus?

M: I'm a captain's character—Captain Mike. I describe my character as a healthy mix of the Skipper from *Gilligan's Island;* Popeye, the sailor man; and Captain Kangaroo.

R: Unmistakable, I would think. Thank you very much for talking with us.

M: Thanks for having me, Robert.

Chapter *13 Social Classes*

FOR THE TEACHER

First Pre-Listening Dictation

1. How would you <u>sum</u> <u>up</u> what it's about?
2. Well, I mean, when you <u>make</u> the kind of money you <u>make</u>, you can <u>no</u> <u>longer</u> be <u>working-class</u>.
3. That's part of the whole <u>class</u> issue that I want to talk about.
4. She <u>has</u> <u>to</u> worry about <u>making</u> ends <u>meet</u>.
5. I was wondering what was <u>behind</u> it.

Second Pre-Listening Dictation

1. How <u>would</u> you sum [<u>it</u>] up?
2. <u>I'd</u> like to make the <u>kind</u> of <u>money</u> he makes.
3. You can no longer be <u>working-class</u>.
4. <u>Making</u> <u>ends</u> meet?
5. What was <u>behind</u> it?

Listen Again to Roseanne

Sentences 2, 5, 8, and 9 are not on the tape.

True or False

1. Roseanne's show is about rich people. (F)
2. Roseanne says that she doesn't worry any more about having enough money. (F)
3. According to Roseanne, it is not difficult to move from one class to another class. (F)
4. Roseanne thinks that you can be rich and also be in the working class. (T)

5. Roseanne has happy memories of her family. (F)

6. Terry Gross has an easy time interviewing Roseanne. (F)

Recycling the Information

1. television show, her autobiography, class, women, rich, working-class

2. disagrees, working-, rich, in the working class

3. money, angry, like, does, work

4. name, husband's, doesn't like

Lecture

A social class is a group of persons in a society that have about the same social standing. Social classes exist because people usually classify one another into groups based on such factors as wealth, power, prestige, education, ancestry, religion, and occupation.

All societies seem to have some system of identifying social class. That is, there are no classless societies. In the United States and other Western democracies, the class system is usually informal, and social scientists disagree on how to classify the groups that seem to exist. Some divide the American people into three classes: upper, middle, and lower. Other social scientists add a fourth class—the working class—between the middle and lower groups, while others substitute the term *working class* for *lower class*.

In the late 1940s, social anthropologist W. Lloyd Warner identified six social classes in a New England community which he studied. Although some sociologists do not agree, these classifications are often used by scholars and the public.

In most Western democracies, persons can move from one class to another, and there are few clear signs as to which group a person belongs. But in some societies, people are born into a certain social class, and it is difficult if not impossible to move into another class. (adapted from *World Book*. 1977. PP448e.)

Questions

1. What would be the best title for this short lecture? (**answer: c**)

2. What does the lecture say about social class in the United States? (**answer: c**)

3. *Who was Mr. W. Lloyd Warner?* **(answer: d)**

4. *According to Mr. Warner, how many social classes were there in the New England community which he studied?* **(answer: c)**

5. *What does the lecture say about social classes in Western democracies?* **(answer: a)**

Transcript

T: How would you sum up what it's [the television show] about?

R: Well, it's a show about class—and women.

T: You know, the interesting thing to me is that as you have gotten more and more successful, I mean wildly successful, your life has gotten further and further away from the life of the Roseanne character in the TV series. I mean—

R: How do you know that?

T: Well, I mean, when you make the kind of money you make, you can no longer be working-class. You can be working, but—

R: Well, does that just mean, does working-class just mean, how much money you make? See, that's part of the whole class issue that I want to talk about and address because that is not true.

T: If it isn't about—

R: It is a culture and that is the culture I was raised in, and that's the culture I portray and will always be a part of no matter what, because that's where I came from and it's who I am.

T: But still, though, I mean your life really has become very different from the Roseanne character's life in the sense that she has to worry about making ends meet and starting a business, periods of unemployment, and stuff like that.

R: So do I.

T: Making ends meet?

R: Yes. Of course. I have a big mortgage and a big house, but I still have to worry about it. I mean, just 'cause it's bigger doesn't mean that all that stuff is gone. And I do have to worry about work and how long it will last and if I'll work again after the show, and, you know, I have the same worries as anybody else, and so do all rich people, and that's just totally ridiculous.

T: Um, I'm wondering—when you married Tom Arnold and you later decided to change your name, I'm wondering why you decided to change your name and I ask that because, first of all, a lot of women don't do it in general anymore, but usually, particularly women in show business whose name has become their public name, even if they change their name in private, they often keep their name in public. So it was an interesting decision on your part and I was wondering what was behind it.

R: I would prefer to have my husband's than my father's [name], because I don't like my father. And I do not like that family, and I don't like that name. And I wanted that period of my life to be over. So when I changed my name to Arnold, I joined a new family.

Chapter *14 A Life-Changing Event*

FOR THE TEACHER

First Pre-Listening Dictation

1. I went to <u>college</u> almost as a bolt <u>out</u> of <u>the</u> blue.
2. I <u>hadn't</u> <u>been</u> doing much of anything.
3. I was <u>hanging</u> <u>out</u> in a local place in Chester, Pennsylvania.
4. He zeroed in on me, and he said, "Are you going to <u>go</u> to <u>college?</u>"
5. It's April; <u>graduation</u> is just down <u>the</u> <u>road</u>.
6. People felt really fairly <u>confident</u> in doing <u>radical</u> things.
7. So the thing that <u>happened</u> was, a man stepped <u>out</u> of <u>nowhere</u> like the hand of <u>God</u>.
8. [They] have their <u>minds</u> made up.
9. Chance and <u>random</u> events played a very big <u>part</u> in my <u>life</u>.

Second Pre-Listening Dictation

1. I hadn't <u>been</u> doing much of <u>anything</u>.
2. I was <u>hanging</u> <u>out</u> in a <u>local</u> place.
3. Graduation is <u>just</u> <u>down</u> the road.
4. He does radical <u>things</u>.
5. [They] <u>have</u> <u>their</u> minds made up.

Listen Again to Brent Staples

Sentences 4 and 9 are not on the tape.

True or False

1. Brent was an excellent student in high school. (F)
2. He was not born into a professional family. (T)

3. He has four brothers and a sister. (F)

4. He had to take preparatory English before he could go to college. (F)

5. He got a job working in the shipyards. (F)

6. He met the black professor when the man came to his school to talk to the senior class. (F)

7. Though he had difficulties in his first year, Brent did well in college. (T)

8. Brent is grateful for the good luck he had. (T)

Recycling the Information

1. in high school, Chester hangout

2. work in Chester, a stranger

3. he hadn't taken the necessary tests, mathematics, black

4. he had difficulties, got excellent grades

5. different, one unexpected event

6. could be better than he was, the *New York Times*

Short Conversations

1. **Man:** I was twenty-four years old when an event changed my life.
   Woman: And what was that life-changing event?
   Man: It was the birth of my baby daughter.

   Question:

   What changed this man's life? (**answer: b**)

2. **Woman:** Let me tell you, on Monday my life suddenly changed.
   Man: What happened?
   Woman: I woke up on Monday morning and decided to buy my first new car.

   Question:

   What did the woman decide to do? (**answer: d**)

3. **Man:** Then something very dramatic happened in my life.
   Woman: What was it?
   Man: I decided to chuck everything and move to Alaska.

   Question:

   What did the man do after he made his big change? **(answer: c)**

4. **Woman:** When did your life change?
   Man: I think the biggest event was graduating from the university.
   Woman: Mine changed the most when I got married.

   Question:

   When did the man's life change? **(answer: d)**

5. **Man:** Tell me about your life-changing event.
   Woman: I never had one.
   Man: What? I find that very difficult to believe.

   Question:

   What has the woman never had? **(answer: a)**

Transcript

Brent: I went to college almost as a bolt out of the blue. It was my senior year in high school. I hadn't been doing much of anything. I hadn't taken the college boards. I was a middling student. I could write well and loved Shakespeare, but I wasn't interested in anything else.

And it was the beginning of spring, my senior year, and I was thinking—well, I'll go and work in the shipyard in Chester, Pennsylvania—the shipyard which is now closed, by the way—and I was hanging out in a local place in Chester, Pennsylvania. And the only black professor from the nearby college was in town doing a survey or something, and he came into our hangout. And he talked with us, just local kids about politics and whatever else we were doing. I was with one of my girlfriends there, who was going to the University of Pennsylvania.

He zeroed in on me, and he said, "Are you going to go to college?"

And I said, "No."

And he said, "Why not?"

I said, "I'm one of nine children. I have to get a job and go to work."

And he said, "You can be better than that."

And I said, "Well, how can I do this? I haven't taken the college boards. It's April; graduation is just down the road. What do I do?"

Remember, this was 1969. This is when colleges had felt that initial mission to integrate the schools. And remember, there were a hundred cities burning every year—between 1964 and 1969—and people felt really fairly confident in doing radical things. He, the professor—his name was Eugene Sparrows, to whom this book is dedicated—got a piece of paper out of his pocket and wrote down the admission director's name, and he said, "Call this man, and tell him I told you to call."

I called, had a long—hour-long—interview, in which I sat on my hands very nervously, and I was accepted to college without having taken college boards. They arranged for me to take them in the fall. I had to take preparatory math courses in the summer. . . . I didn't need English, but preparatory math courses.

And I stumbled at first. But very soon, I was near the top of my class. So the thing that happened was, a man stepped out of nowhere, like the hand of God, in Chester, Pennsylvania, on a bad street corner, and said, "You can be better."

Terry: Now, if this man had not interceded in an almost godlike way, you probably would have gotten a job at the shipyard and would not have written a book or become an editorial writer. You would not probably have entered the professional class, so to speak.

Brent: Exactly. I have been very fortunate. And one of the things I talk about often, what annoys me as a journalist—when I have my journalist hat on—is that people will ask the question: What's the difference between your brother and you? they'll say. And many of those people, many people, who ask that question have their minds made up. You see, they think it's a matter of constitution—personal constitution—or they think it's a matter of sort of basic goodness or Horatio Alger–ness. And they find it difficult when I explain to them that chance and random events played a very big part in my life. And they play a big part in everyone's life.

Acknowledgments and Credits *(continued from p. ii)*

Ch. 3, p. 19: Jane Brody, courtesy of Jane Brody, the *New York Times*.

Ch. 5, p. 40: Alan Shepard on the moon, NASA; **p. 45:** Earth as pictured from moon, NASA.

Ch. 7, p. 60: Postman walking his route in the summer, Irene Bayer/Monkmeyer.

Ch. 8, p. 68: Jimmy Carter in Haiti, AP/Wide World Photos.

Ch. 9, p. 77: Traffic jam in Tokyo. Ira Kirschenbaum/Stock, Boston.

Ch. 10, p. 87: Rosalynn Carter, official photo, UPI/Corbis-Bettmann;
p. 92: Rosalynn and Jimmy Carter building houses at Habitat for Humanity, UPI/Corbis-Bettmann.

Ch. 11, p. 95 top: Man doing dishes, Robert Finken/The Picture Cube;
p. 95 bottom: Japanese-American woman architect, Spencer Grant/Photo Researchers; **p. 99:** Teenager doing laundry, Michael Dwyer/Stock, Boston.

Ch. 12, p. 103: Guenther Goebbel-Williams training lions, AP/Wide World Photos;
p. 107: Ringling Brothers clown college, AP/Wide World Photos.

Ch. 13, p. 113: Roseanne Barr on the set of *Roseanne,* PHOTOFEST;
p. 118: Roseanne Barr at book signing, AP/Wide World Photos.

Ch. 14, p. 121: Brent Staples as NYT editorial writer today, courtesy of Brent Staples, © 1994 Lisa Spindle; **p. 128:** Brent Staples from his high school yearbook, courtesy of Brent Staples.

P. 134: Tom and Ray Magliozzi (Click and Clack) from NPR *Car Talk,* courtesy of National Public Radio.

P. 139: Boy riding bike, Paris, Jaye R. Phillips/The Picture Cube.

P. 144: Jane Brody, courtesy of Jane Brody, the *New York Times*.

P. 155: Alan Shepard on the moon, NASA.

P. 165: Postman walking his route in the summer, Irene Bayer/Monkmeyer.

P. 172: Jimmy Carter in Haiti, AP/Wide World Photos.

P. 177: Traffic jam in Tokyo. Ira Kirschenbaum/Stock, Boston.

P. 183: Rosalynn Carter, official photo, UPI/Corbis-Bettmann.

P. 188 top: Man doing dishes, Robert Finken/The Picture Cube;
p. 188 bottom: Japanese-American woman architect, Spencer Grant/Photo Researchers.

P. 194: Guenther Goebbel-Williams training lions, AP/Wide World Photos.

P. 200: Roseanne Barr on the set of *Roseanne,* PHOTOFEST.

P. 205: Brent Staples as NYT editorial writer today, Courtesy of Brent Staples, © 1994 Lisa Spindle.

Text Credits

Car Talk, with program hosts Click and Clack. Broadcast on Vermont National Public Radio, August 14, 1993. Reproduced by permission of Dewey, Cheetham, and Howe, producers of *Car Talk*®.

Talk of the Nation, with program host Robert Siegel: excerpts from "Taking Time Off," (September 30, 1992), "Are You Game?," (February 14, 1995), "Parking in Tokyo," by T. R Reid, with special permission by the author, (July 28, 1991), and "Chucking It All," (September 30, 1992). Broadcast on National Public Radio. Reproduced with permission.

Fresh Air, with program host Terry Gross. Produced by WHYNN-FM radio station, Philadelphia, Pennsylvania, distributed by National Public Radio. All rights reserved. Reproduced by permission. Excerpts from "Standing on the Moon," (Alan Shepard), "Former President Jimmy Carter," "Rosalynn Carter, Former First Lady," and "Social Classes," (Roseanne). Excerpts from "The Common Cold," (Jane Brody) from *Jane Brody's Cold and Flu Fighter.* Copyright © 1995 by Jane Brody. Published by W. W. Norton & Co. Reproduced by permission of the publisher and the author. Excerpts from "A Life-Changing Event," (Brent Staples). Brent Staples is the author of the memoir *Parallel Time: Growing Up in Black and White,* published by Pantheon (hc., 1994) and Avon (pb., 1995), and writes editorials for the *New York Times.*

Cellular Mobile Communications ad. Reproduced by permission of Philip DePalma, President & CEO, Cellular Mobile Communications, Inc., Woburn, MA.

Northwest Airlines radio ad. Reproduced by permission of Rick Dow, Northwest Airlines.

Radio Talk, with program host Jerry Williams. AM 680 WRKO The Talk Station, Boston, Massachusetts, a division of American Radio Systems Corporation. Reproduced by permission. Excerpts from "Labor Day," (1993) with guest host Steve Weisman. "Husbands and Wives," with guest Shirley Sloane Fader. *You Can Have It All,* 3rd revised ed. by Arnold M. Patent. Published by Beyond Words Publishing, Inc., Hillsboro, Oregon. (503-693-8700; email: BeyondWord@qol.com).